D1288699

Worldwide Security Under the "Prince of Peace"

Worldwide security under the "Prince of Peace" is an absolute certainty. The Almighty God assures us of this in the prophecy about the birth and career of the "Prince of Peace" at Isaiah 9:6, 7: "His name will be called . . . Prince of Peace. To the abundance of the princely rule and to peace there will be no end . . . The very zeal of Jehovah of armies will do this." How readers of this book can prepare to enter into the abundance of the rule of the "Prince of Peace" is set forth in this volume.

—The Publishers.

Copyright © 1986 by
WATCH TOWER BIBLE AND TRACT SOCIETY
OF PENNSYLVANIA
INTERNATIONAL BIBLE STUDENTS
ASSOCIATION

Publishers
WATCHTOWER BIBLE AND TRACT SOCIETY
OF NEW YORK, INC.
INTERNATIONAL BIBLE STUDENTS ASSOCIATION
Brooklyn, New York, U.S.A.

First Edition
6,000,000 copies
25 languages

Bible quotations in this book are from the *New World Translation of the Holy Scriptures,* 1984 edition.

Worldwide Security Under the "Prince of Peace"
English (ws-E)

Made in the United States of America

Contents

Chapter 1

The Desire for Peace and Security Worldwide

PEACE and security are what we want here on earth. The need for such a desirable situation was never more pressing than it is today. This is true not only with us as individuals but also with the entire human family around the globe.

[2] That is why the present population of earth is now living in the time of all times! 'How can this be the case,' you may ask, 'since we are now well along in the most frightful period of all human history, the age of nuclear weapons?'

[3] At least eight nations are reported to be capable of producing the nuclear bomb. And it is estimated that 31 countries could have nuclear weap-

1, 2. What pressing need does all mankind have, and why?
3. (a) What is said to be the reason for the nations' possessing the nuclear bomb? (b) What would ordinary common sense dictate?

The Creator has his own perfect way for satisfying human desire for peace and security

ons by the year 2000. Their reason for possessing the ultimate of bombs is said to be that of protection, a deterrent to other similarly armed nations, a threat of nuclear reprisal. In the face of such a state of world affairs, ordinary common sense would dictate that the nations should agree to live side by side in mutual tolerance.

[4] Is it, however, a mere man-made peace that we want, together with what security man can pro-

4. Though the Creator has not blocked human efforts to seek security, what purpose does he have in this regard?

vide? Though the Creator has not blocked human efforts to establish and maintain peace and security worldwide, he has his own perfect way for satisfying our natural desire for peace and security. He has his own appointed time for doing away with all disturbers of the security of those who desire to worship him. How glad we can be to know that his time for this is at hand!

5 After thousands of years of turbulent human history, it is to be expected that there should be an intense earth-wide desire for peace and security. Earth has been man's natural habitat from the very start of human existence. The inspired psalmist said: "As regards the heavens, to Jehovah the heavens belong, but the earth he has given to the sons of men." (Psalm 115:16) From the very beginning, it was the Creator's loving purpose that man should enjoy a full life in his God-given earthly home.

6 According to the creation account at Genesis 2:7, "God proceeded to form the man out of dust from the ground and to blow into his nostrils the breath of life, and the man came to be a living soul." No other living creature on earth was on man's plane of life or on man's level of competence—able to act like God in the exercise of dominion. Further, this dominion was not to be confined to the first human creature but was also to be exercised and enjoyed by his offspring.

---

5. What did the inspired psalmist say regarding the earth, and what is the Creator's purpose for man?

6. In what respect would the first man and his offspring be able to act like God?

7 For that reason, the Creator gave Adam a wife. She was to be the mother of all future human inhabitants of earth. That is why, on being presented with this perfect creature, the man could say: "This is at last bone of my bones and flesh of my flesh." Therefore he pronounced her the female of the human kind, *'ish·shah',* which is the feminine form of the Hebrew word translated man, namely, *'ish.*—Genesis 2:21-23.

8 The Creator and heavenly Father said to the first human couple: "Be fruitful and become many and fill the earth and subdue it." (Genesis 1:28) This procedure was something absolutely new in the history of intelligent creation. The spiritual inhabitants of the invisible heavens were not brought into existence through procreation.

9 It is no wonder that, at the time of earth's creation, "the morning stars joyfully cried out together, and all the sons of God began shouting in applause." (Job 38:7) At that time, all was peaceful and harmonious throughout the entire universe. In the eighth psalm, enraptured at the divine arrangement of things, the psalmist exclaims regarding man: "You also proceeded to make him a little less than godlike ones, and with glory and splendor you then crowned him." (Verses 4, 5) According to this psalm, God put all things here on earth under man's feet.

---

7. How did Adam come to have a wife, and what did he say when this perfect creature was presented to him?
8. What instructions did the Creator give to the first human couple?
9. How does Psalm 8:4, 5 describe the divine arrangement of things?

The Start of a Rival Sovereignty

[10] Amazingly, before the first human child was conceived, rebellion broke out in the universal organization of Jehovah God. The situation could lead to the setting up of a new sovereignty, a new superrulership, over humankind—if humankind could be separated and alienated from Jehovah's universal organization. A sovereignty could be set up in rivalry to his. This called for the first lie to be told, presenting Jehovah God in a false light.

[11] The telling of the first falsehood made this first rebel against God the first liar, the first devil, or defamer. In stark contrast to him, Jesus Christ said: "I am the way and the truth and the life." (John 14:6) To his religious opposers, Jesus said: "You are from your father the Devil, and you wish to do the desires of your father. That one was a manslayer when he began, and he did not stand fast in the truth, because truth is not in him. When he speaks the lie, he speaks according to his own disposition, because he is a liar and the father of the lie."—John 8:44.

[12] By speaking through a serpent in the garden of Eden, or paradise of pleasure, the Devil caused the first lie to be presented to the first woman. He claimed that her Creator was a liar, thus disturbing the peace of Eve's mind. He made her feel a

---

10. (a) Before the first human child was conceived, what broke out? (b) What could thus be set up over humankind?
11. By presenting Jehovah God in a false light, what did the first rebel become?
12. (a) How did the Devil cause the first lie to be told, and what was the effect upon Eve? (b) What resulted when Adam ate of the forbidden fruit?

sense of insecurity in her imagined state of ignorance, so she partook of the forbidden fruit. She prevailed upon her husband, Adam, to partake of the forbidden fruit with her and thus join her in her rebellion against Jehovah God. (Genesis 3:1-6) The disobedient couple lost their peace with God and were driven out of the paradise of pleasure to exist in a state of insecurity outside. Romans 5:12 describes this sorry state of affairs, saying: "Through one man sin entered into the world and death through sin, and thus death spread to all men because they had all sinned."

[13] The situation of our day calls for us to make a definite choice. It is a choice between the rival sovereignty of Satan the Devil, "the god of this system of things," and the sovereignty of Jehovah, the Most High and Almighty God of the universe.—2 Corinthians 4:4; Psalm 83:18.

The Way to Enjoy Peace With God

[14] With painful hurt to themselves, most of mankind do not desire to accept or to believe in the Almighty God's provision for his worshipers to enjoy relative peace and security even in this most lamentable state of human affairs. However, Jehovah is "the God who gives peace," and it is our blessed privilege now to enter into a peace and security that will never fail. (Romans 16:20; Philippians 4:6, 7, 9) It is a peace and security that he gives even now to his body of earthly servants, his visible organization, in fulfillment of his ever-

---

13. What choice must each of us make today?
14. What peace and security can we begin to enjoy even now?

reliable promises. It is a peace and security that we can enjoy only in association with his visible organization on earth.

[15] It would be out of line with the plain teachings of the Scriptures to believe that God does not have an organization, an organized people, that he exclusively recognizes. Jesus Christ recognized that his heavenly Father had a visible organization. Until Pentecost 33 C.E., it was the Jewish organization in covenant relationship with Jehovah God under the Law of Moses.—Luke 16:16.

[16] Just as the ancient nation of Israel was in a covenant relationship with Jehovah God through the mediator Moses, so the nation of spiritual Israel, "the Israel of God," has a covenant relationship through a mediator. (Galatians 6:16) It is as the apostle Paul wrote to his Christian fellow worker: "There is one God, and one mediator between God and men, a man, Christ Jesus." (1 Timothy 2:5) Was Moses the mediator between Jehovah God and mankind in general? No, he was the mediator between the God of Abraham, Isaac, and Jacob and the nation of their fleshly descendants. Likewise, the Greater Moses, Jesus Christ, is not the Mediator between Jehovah God and all mankind. He is the Mediator between his heavenly Father, Jehovah God, and the nation of spiritual Israel, which is limited to only 144,000 members.

---

15. Is it unreasonable to think that God has an organization, and what did Jesus Christ recognize?

16. (a) Between whom was Moses the mediator? (b) Between whom is the Greater Moses, Jesus Christ, the Mediator?

This spiritual nation is like a little flock of Jehovah's sheeplike ones.—Romans 9:6; Revelation 7:4.

Shepherd Over More Than the "Little Flock"

[17] In Psalm 23:1, King David of ancient Israel was inspired to say: "Jehovah is my Shepherd. I shall lack nothing." Jehovah, the Supreme Shepherd, has assigned Jesus Christ to be "the fine shepherd." (John 10:11) At Luke 12:32, Jesus addressed himself to those of whom he is the Fine Shepherd: "Have no fear, little flock, because your Father has approved of giving you the kingdom."

[18] In ancient times, there were non-Jews, such as the Nethinim and the sons of non-Israelite servants of Solomon, who were associated with the nation of Israel. (Ezra 2:43-58; 8:17-20) Similarly today, there are men and women who are wholly dedicated to God through Jesus Christ but who are not spiritual Israelites. They are, however, associated with the remnant of spiritual Israel because of dedicating themselves to Jehovah God through Jesus Christ, "who gave himself a corresponding ransom for all." (1 Timothy 2:6) Today, these far outnumber the 144,000 spiritual Israelites, who are to inherit the heavenly Kingdom.

---

17. (a) What has Jehovah God assigned Jesus Christ to be? (b) What did Jesus say to those who are to inherit the heavenly Kingdom?

18. (a) Who today correspond to the Nethinim and the sons of non-Israelite servants of Solomon? (b) With whom are they closely associated?

[19] Thus Jesus Christ was to be assigned, in God's due time, to be the Shepherd over a much larger flock of sheeplike ones who would come into an earthly inheritance through him. These are the ones whom he had in mind when he said: "I have other sheep, which are not of this fold; those also I must bring, and they will listen to my voice, and they will become one flock, one shepherd." Having in mind these "other sheep," the apostle John also wrote of Jesus: "He is a propitiatory sacrifice for our sins, yet not for ours only but also for the whole world's."—John 10:16; 1 John 2:2.

[20] Today, there are about 9,000 who profess to be members of the remnant of the "little flock" of spiritual sheep. On the other hand, there are millions of dedicated ones who are associated with the anointed remnant in following in the footsteps of the Fine Shepherd, Jesus Christ. They are to be found in over 200 lands around the globe. What does the pastoral care of that Fine Shepherd mean for all of them? It means the enjoyment of peace and security! If they did not have peace in their ranks, there would not be heartfelt unity and unbreakable cooperation among them. If they did not have mutual loving concern for one another as respects spiritual interests, they would not have the security that they enjoy. Thus, their desire for peace and security earth wide has begun to be satisfied even now.

---

19. What did Jesus Christ say to indicate that he would be the Shepherd over more than the "little flock"?
20. (a) How does the number of the "other sheep" compare with that of the remaining ones of the "little flock"? (b) What does the pastoral care of the Fine Shepherd mean for all of them?

Chapter 2

The "Prince of Peace" Faces Armageddon

IN THE eighth century before our Common Era, the prophet Isaiah was inspired to say to God's people: "For there has been a child born to us, there has been a son given to us; and the princely rule will come to be upon his shoulder. And his name will be called Wonderful Counselor, Mighty God, Eternal Father, Prince of Peace. To the abundance of the princely rule and to peace there will be no end, upon the throne of David and upon his kingdom in order to establish it firmly and to sustain it by means of justice and by means of righteousness, from now on and to time indefinite."—Isaiah 9:6, 7.

2 Those thrilling words began to be fulfilled in the latter part of the year 2 B.C.E. This was when Jesus was born as a descendant of King David, who had reigned in the city of Jerusalem over the 12 tribes of Israel.

Covenant for a Kingdom With No End of Peace

3 Because of David's zeal for the worship of the

1, 2. (a) What thrilling words did God inspire the prophet Isaiah to speak? (b) When did these words begin to be fulfilled?

3. (a) What covenant did God make with King David? (b) Upon what descendant of King David has Jehovah conferred the title "Prince of Peace"?

God of Israel, Jehovah made with him a covenant for an everlasting Kingdom in his line of descent. (2 Samuel 7:1-16) That covenant was backed by God's oath. (Psalm 132:11, 12) According to that covenant, David's kingdom had to furnish the basis for the coming Kingdom of the "Prince of Peace." "Jesus Christ, son of David," is the one upon whom Jehovah conferred the title "Prince of Peace."—Matthew 1:1.

4 Jesus' mother was a woman born into the royal line of King David. She was a virgin when she conceived her promised son, who would become the permanent heir to David's throne. This conception took place before Joseph took her as his wife. (Matthew 1:18-25) The angel Gabriel had informed the virgin Mary: "Look! you will conceive in your womb and give birth to a son, and you are to call his name Jesus. This one will be great and will be called Son of the Most High; and Jehovah God will give him the throne of David his father, and he will rule as king over the house of Jacob forever, and there will be no end of his kingdom."—Luke 1:31-33.

5 That is why the prophet Isaiah foretold regarding the "Prince of Peace" that "wide is his dominion in a peace that has no end, for the throne of David and for his royal power." (Isaiah 9:6, 7, *The Jerusalem Bible*) Thus, according to the covenant established with David, this King-

---

4. (a) Who became the earthly mother of Jesus? (b) What did the angel Gabriel say to her in this respect?
5. What had Isaiah the prophet foretold regarding the rule of the "Prince of Peace"?

dom would be an everlasting government with no end of peace. His throne must stand "forever"!

[6] For the carrying out of this Kingdom covenant, the Almighty God resurrected Jesus from the dead on the third day of his martyrdom. This was on the 16th day of the Jewish month Nisan, in the year 33 of our Common Era. As an eyewitness of the resurrected Son of God, the apostle Peter said that Jesus was "put to death in the flesh, but . . . made alive in the spirit." (1 Peter 3:18) The Most High God elevated him to His own right hand. There, since the end of the Gentile Times, or "the appointed times of the nations," in early October of the year 1914, he has been reigning as the "Prince of Peace."—Luke 21:24.

[7] From the start of his celestial reign, he has faced a hostile world, as is evidenced by two world wars over the issue of who shall rule the earth. He is now confronted with the United Nations organization. By the globe-encircling proclamation of the good news of the Kingdom by Jehovah's Witnesses, who are preaching in more than 200 lands, his active kingship in the heavens is being called to the attention of all nations. This is in fulfillment of what the "Prince of Peace" himself foretold, as we read at Matthew 24:14: "This good news of the kingdom will be preached

---

6. (a) To carry out the Kingdom covenant, what did God do on the third day of Jesus' death? (b) When did Jesus begin to reign as the "Prince of Peace"?

7. (a) What has Jesus faced from the start of his reign? (b) Who are proclaiming Jesus' kingship to all the nations, and in fulfillment of what?

in all the inhabited earth for a witness to all the nations; and then the end will come."

[8] The issue of world domination must be settled soon. Now, more than 70 years after the end of "the appointed times of the nations" in 1914, we are deep into this "conclusion of the system of things." The generation of 1914 saw the start of the meaningful world events foretold by Jesus. (Matthew 24:3-14) That generation, Jesus said, would not pass away until all these things would be fulfilled. It is now very close to finishing its course.—Matthew 24:34.

[9] Hence, what lies immediately ahead, and what does the "Prince of Peace" face? He himself was used to foretell this in the very last book of the Bible, the Revelation, or Apocalypse, which God gave to him and which he communicated to the aged apostle John by means of an angel. (Revelation 1:1, 2) That happened about the end of the first century of our Common Era. At Revelation 16:13, 14, 16, Jesus had the apostle John make this significant reference to Har–Magedon, or Armageddon:

[10] "And I saw three unclean inspired expressions that looked like frogs come out of the mouth of the dragon and out of the mouth of the wild beast and out of the mouth of the false prophet. They are, in fact, expressions inspired

---

8. Why can it be said that we are very deep into this "conclusion of the system of things"?

9, 10. (a) How was the prophetic information in the book of Revelation communicated to us? (b) What does Revelation 16:13, 14, 16 foretell about Har–Magedon, or Armageddon?

by demons and perform signs, and they go forth to the kings of the entire inhabited earth, to gather them together to the war of the great day of God the Almighty. And they gathered them together to the place that is called in Hebrew Har–Magedon."

The Figurative "Mountain of Megiddo"

11 The Hebrew name Har–Magedon, or Armageddon, means "Mountain of Megiddo." No geographical location in ancient or modern times has been called Mountain of Megiddo. Thus in a book like Revelation that is filled with figurative language, the term has symbolic meaning. What must that be? Well, the elevated city of Megiddo, the name of which place means "assembly of troops," was of historical importance. In secular and in Biblical history the name stirred up memories of decisive battles. Why? Because the city then dominated a strategic land passageway between Europe, Asia, and Africa, and invaders could advantageously be challenged and halted there by the inhabitants. Thus Megiddo took on a double meaning—that of tragic defeat for one side and of glorious victory for the other side.

12 The God of the Bible became associated with

11. (a) What does the name Armageddon mean, and was there ever a geographical location so named? (b) Why was the ancient city of Megiddo of historical importance? (c) What double meaning did the name Megiddo take on?

12, 13. (a) How did the God of the Bible become associated with Megiddo and its nearby river during the days of Judge Barak? (b) How does the victory song of Barak and Deborah describe God's role in the victory?

Megiddo and with the nearby river Kishon during the period of the Israelite judges. In the days of Judge Barak and the prophetess Deborah, God gave a signal victory to his chosen people in the neighborhood of Megiddo. Judge Barak had only 10,000 men, whereas the enemy under General Sisera had, besides ground troops, 900 horse-drawn war chariots. Jehovah stepped into the battle in behalf of his chosen people and caused a flash flood to immobilize those formidable chariots of the enemy. In the victory song that Barak and Deborah sang to God after the miraculous defeat of Sisera's army, they called attention to God's part in this overthrow of the enemy:

[13] "Kings came, they fought; it was then that the kings of Canaan fought in Taanach by the waters of Megiddo. No gain of silver did they take. From heaven did the stars fight, from their orbits they fought against Sisera. The torrent of Kishon washed them away, the torrent of ancient days, the torrent of Kishon."—Judges 5:12, 19-21.

[14] Without doubt, the inspired words with which Barak and Deborah closed their song after that ancient victory at Megiddo apply as a prayer with regard to the coming war at Armageddon. They sang: "Thus let all your enemies perish, O Jehovah, and let your lovers be as when the sun goes forth in its mightiness."—Judges 5:31.*

* Some other references to Megiddo are found at 2 Kings 9:27; 23:29, 30; 2 Chronicles 35:22; Zechariah 12:11.

14. What closing words of that inspired victory song are no doubt a prayer with regard to the coming war at Armageddon?

Nations Being Gathered to Armageddon

15 So Megiddo was a place where decisive battles were fought. Logically, then, Armageddon would be the battlefield to which all the worldly nations of today would march under the inciting forces described at Revelation 16:13, 14. The "expressions inspired by demons" that mobilize the nations are the propaganda that is today croaked forth, unclean like the Biblically unclean frog. One of the sources of such unclean propaganda is the "great fiery-colored dragon." Revelation 12:1-9 identifies "the dragon" as Satan the Devil.

16 Another source of unclean propaganda is "the wild beast." At Revelation 16:13 this symbolic "wild beast" is associated with the devilish "dragon." According to Revelation 20:10, this "wild beast" will be destroyed forever because of its cooperation with the symbolic "dragon." "The wild beast" symbolizes the entire political system of this world of which "the dragon" is the god. (2 Corinthians 4:4) It takes in all the various political governments of this world.—Compare Daniel 7:17; 8:20, 22.

17 Such a world system of political rule has its distinctive propaganda. And this croaking, froglike propaganda is an inspired expression that serves with the inspired expression of "the dragon" to gather "the kings," or political rulers of the

---

15. (a) What kind of place, then, is Armageddon? (b) What is one of the sources of the unclean propaganda that mobilizes the nations to the war at Armageddon?
16. At Revelation 16:13, what does "the wild beast" symbolize?
17. What is the effect of the froglike propaganda issuing forth from "the wild beast"?

world, to "the war of the great day of God the Almighty" that will be fought at Armageddon.

[18] Har–Magedon thus signifies a world situation that involves a decisive war. It denotes that ultimate state to which world affairs come where the political rulers unitedly oppose God's will, so that God must react with a counterforce according to his purpose. So the future is to be determined by what results from this confrontation. At Megiddo itself, the geographical location, there was no mountain. But a mountain would symbolize a prominent place of assembly that would be easily discerned from a distance by all the military forces gathering there.

[19] Jesus Christ, the General of Jehovah's fighting forces, has for some years looked upon the gathering of the rulers of the world and their fighting forces to Armageddon. But he has not tried to single out any particular king and his military forces to strike them down singly and thus finish off the enemy forces piecemeal. On the contrary, he is allowing them sufficient time to mass together and to unify their forces to the greatest military potential. His bold purpose is to take all of them on at the same time!

[20] He will thereby gain a more resounding victory over them, to the glory of his own Commander in Chief, Jehovah God, and to the verification of himself as, indisputably, the "King of kings and Lord of lords."—Revelation 19:16.

---

18. (a) What does the name Har–Magedon denote? (b) What would a mountain symbolize?

19, 20. What strategy will the General of Jehovah's heavenly forces use at Armageddon, and with what result?

Chapter 3

The Rule of the "Prince of Peace" Amid Enemies

SHORTLY before his ascension to heaven more than 19 centuries ago, the then future "Prince of Peace," Jesus Christ, said these parting words to a group of his faithful disciples: "Go therefore and make disciples of people of all the nations, baptizing them in the name of the Father and of the Son and of the holy spirit . . . And, look! I am with you all the days until the conclusion of the system of things."—Matthew 28:19, 20.

2 Did those words of Jesus call for world conversion before "the conclusion of the system of things" that began in 1914? No. Today, near the close of this 20th century, the world of mankind remains far from being converted to Jesus Christ as its Savior and rightful King. However, this has not delayed the outworking of what Jehovah foretold in the prophecies of the Bible. It was never God's purpose that the whole world of mankind be converted before Jesus Christ began to rule as the "Prince of Peace." Directly contrary, he was foretold to begin ruling in the midst of his enemies.

1, 2. (a) What parting words did Jesus Christ say to a group of his disciples? (b) Did this call for world conversion before he would rule as the "Prince of Peace"?

[3] Even when he was down here on earth, Jesus Christ knew this fact. Shortly before his death as a martyr, he had a dispute with his religious opposers and made a reference to Psalm 110. We read about this at Luke 20:41-44: "In turn he said to them: 'How is it they say that the Christ is David's son? For David himself says in the book of Psalms, "Jehovah said to my Lord, Sit at my right hand until I place your enemies as a stool for your feet." David, therefore, calls him "Lord"; so how is he his son?'"

[4] Plainly, then, Jesus Christ, as the Son of David, was not to begin ruling after world conversion. Rather, he was to begin ruling among enemies whom Jehovah God by warfare would eventually make the footstool for the feet of his enthroned Son. Psalm 2 likewise, in the following words, indicates the beginning of his rule as the "Prince of Peace" amid enemies:

[5] "Why have the nations been in tumult and the national groups themselves kept muttering an empty thing? The kings of earth take their stand and high officials themselves have massed together as one against Jehovah and against his anointed one [his Christ], saying: 'Let us tear their bands apart and cast their cords away from us!' The very One sitting in the heavens will laugh; Jehovah himself will hold them in derision. At

---

3. How did Jesus' reference to Psalm 110 indicate that he would reign amid enemies?

4-6. (a) How does Psalm 2 likewise indicate that Jesus would not have to wait for world conversion before beginning his rule as the "Prince of Peace"? (b) At what time was Psalm 2:7 fulfilled?

that time he will speak to them in his anger and in his hot displeasure he will disturb them, saying: 'I, even I, have installed my king upon Zion, my holy mountain.'

6 "Let me refer to the decree of Jehovah; he has said to me [Christ]: 'You are my son; I, today, I have become your father. [Psalm 2:7 was fulfilled when Jehovah resurrected his Son from the dead, thus becoming an everlasting Father to Jesus. (Romans 1:4)] Ask of me, that I may give nations as your inheritance and the ends of the earth as your own possession. You will break them with an iron scepter, as though a potter's vessel you will dash them to pieces.' And now, O kings, exercise insight; let yourselves be corrected, O judges of the earth. Serve Jehovah with fear and be joyful with trembling. Kiss the son, that He may not become incensed and you may not perish from the way, for his anger flares up easily. Happy are all those taking refuge in him."

7 According to Acts 4:24-27, the apostles of Jesus Christ referred to this second psalm after the day of Pentecost, 33 C.E.: "They with one accord raised their voices to God and said: 'Sovereign Lord, you are the One who made the heaven and the earth and the sea and all the things in them, and who through holy spirit said by the mouth of our forefather David, your servant, "Why did nations become tumultuous and peoples meditate upon empty things? The kings of the earth took their stand and the rulers massed together as one

---

7. What reference to Psalm 2 did the apostles of Jesus Christ make after the day of Pentecost?

against Jehovah and against his anointed one." Even so, both Herod and Pontius Pilate with men of nations and with peoples of Israel were in actuality gathered together in this city against your holy servant Jesus, whom you anointed.'"

Major Fulfillment of Psalm 2

8 The year 33 of the first century saw the first fulfillment of those prophetic words of Psalm 2: 1, 2. This was in connection with the man Jesus Christ on earth. He had been anointed with Jehovah's holy spirit at the time of his baptism by John the Baptizer. But the major fulfillment of Psalm 2 has been taking place since the end of the Gentile Times in the year 1914. (Luke 21:24) It has been amply verified that "the appointed times of the nations," which began at the first destruction of the city of Jerusalem in 607 B.C.E., ended in the year 1914.* Then the death knell sounded for the nations of this world, including those of Christendom.

9 At the first destruction of Jerusalem, by the Babylonians, the Kingdom of Jehovah God over the nation of Israel, as represented by the royal line of King David, came to an end. Since then, the natural Jews have not had a king over them in

---

* For details, see the book *You Can Live Forever in Paradise on Earth,* pages 138-41, published by the Watchtower Bible and Tract Society of New York, Inc.

---

8. (a) When did the first fulfillment of Psalm 2:1, 2 take place? (b) Since when has the major fulfillment of Psalm 2 been taking place?
9. What happened at the first destruction of Jerusalem with regard to the Kingdom of God as represented by the royal line of King David?

the line of the royal house of David. But the Kingdom of the Most High God in the hands of a descendant of David, with whom Jehovah made a covenant for an everlasting Kingdom in his line, was not to lie prone on earth forever.

[10] To the king of ancient Jerusalem, shortly before its first destruction, Jehovah caused his prophet Ezekiel to direct these words: "As for you, O deadly wounded, wicked chieftain of Israel, whose day has come in the time of the error of the end, this is what the Sovereign Lord Jehovah has said, 'Remove the turban, and lift off the crown. This will not be the same. Put on high even what is low, and bring low even the high one. A ruin, a ruin, a ruin I shall make it. As for this also, it will certainly become no one's until he comes who has the legal right, and I must give it to him.'"—Ezekiel 21:25-27.

[11] The one with "the legal right" came in the person of Jesus Christ, and his line of descent from David is recorded at Matthew 1:1-16 and Luke 3:23-31. He was generally addressed as "the Son of David." On the day of his triumphal ride into Jerusalem, mounted on an ass in fulfillment of prophecy, the exulting crowd of Jews that accompanied him and his apostles cried out jubilantly: "Save, we pray, the Son of David! Blessed is he that comes in Jehovah's name! Save him, we pray, in the heights above!"—Matthew 21:9.

10, 11. (a) What did God through his prophet Ezekiel say with regard to the throne of David? (b) Who came with "the legal right" to David's throne? (c) What did the crowd of Jews say when he presented himself as the legal heir?

"The Son of David" Is Enthroned in Heaven

12 The 2,520 years for the Gentiles to be treading underfoot the Kingdom of God in the hands of the house of David ended in 1914. Then came the time for Jesus Christ, "the Son of David," to be enthroned, not down here on an earthly throne, but in the highest heavens at the right hand of Jehovah God!—Daniel 7:9, 10, 13, 14.

13 That momentous date had been pointed forward to since 1876 by those who became associated with the Watch Tower Bible and Tract Society. But the nations of the earth, even those of Christendom, refused to recognize it as the time for them to turn over their earthly sovereignties to the newly enthroned "Son of David." They did not acknowledge that he held the God-given right to sovereignty over the whole earth, which is Jehovah God's footstool. (Matthew 5:35) They signalized their flagrant rejection of the rightful King by engaging in the first world war.

14 In all the warring nations, the dedicated Christians who were associated with the Watch Tower Society came under tremendous pressure

---

12. When the Gentile Times ended in 1914, where was Jesus Christ, as David's permanent heir, enthroned?
13. (a) Since what date was the year 1914 pointed forward to as the end of the Gentile Times, and by whom? (b) What was the attitude of the nations of the earth toward the newly enthroned "Son of David"?
14. (a) With the outbreak of World War I, what attitude did the nations manifest toward those Christians associated with the Watch Tower Society? (b) In view of this, what does the worldwide situation signify?

to abandon their resolve to keep free from bloodguilt. They did not then understand to the fullest degree the requirement for Christian neutrality. The prophecy of "the Son of David," Jesus Christ, to his disciples regarding "the conclusion of the system of things" came painfully true: "You will be objects of hatred by all the nations on account of my name." (Matthew 24:9) This hatred has not abated since the end of World War I. In view of these meaningful facts of modern history, what does the worldwide situation signify? This: The "Prince of Peace" rules amid enemies who are right here on earth!

15 The Almighty God brought the promised Messianic Kingdom to birth at his appointed time in spite of all the enemies that were on hand in heaven and on earth. Revelation 12:1-9 shows that after the birth of 'the man-child' Kingdom in the heavens from the womb of Jehovah's wifelike organization, as it were, warfare promptly broke out in heaven itself. The holy heavens were no longer the place for the symbolic dragon, Satan the Devil, and his demonic angels. In this warfare, unseen to human eyes, the royally empowered "Son of David" fought victoriously and ejected Satan the Devil and his demon hordes from the heavens and confined them to the vicinity of our earthly globe. This debasement of the satanic forces was evidently fully accomplished by 1918, the year when World War I came to an end.

---

15. What happened to Satan the Devil and his demon hordes when warfare broke out in heaven, and by what year must the results have been conclusive?

Demoted, the Devil Wages War

[16] The demoted Satan the Devil, the symbolic dragon, is now especially wrathful toward the wifelike organization of Jehovah God. (Revelation 12:17) Thus he viciously wages warfare upon the spirit-begotten remnant of dedicated Christians who have the evidence that she is their spiritual mother.—Galatians 4:26.

[17] Satan also wages war on the "other sheep," who obediently work with the anointed remnant in bearing witness to the Kingdom's birth. (John 10:16) He not only uses his demoted demon forces, now in the vicinity of the earth, but also employs the visible part of his organization to carry on this warfare against the remnant and the "other sheep."

[18] The rule of the "Prince of Peace" amid his enemies down here at the earth nears its close. He has taken excellent care of the situation. Day and night his loyal holy angels stand at attention, ready to receive royal orders from him and to act upon them with dispatch. They serve as a protective force for the anointed remnant and their companions, the "great crowd" of "other sheep," as these continue to serve the Kingdom interests during this fast-diminishing time when the "Prince of Peace" rules amid his enemies.—Revelation 7:9.

16, 17. (a) Against whom does the demoted Satan the Devil wage warfare? (b) Whom does he use to carry on this warfare?
18. (a) Though the Devil viciously wages war against the anointed remnant and their companions, what protective force do they have? (b) What aspect of the rule of the "Prince of Peace" nears its end?

Chapter 4

Insecure "Babylon" Doomed to Destruction

CONFUSION marks the world today—politically, socially, and religiously. The English translation of the Bible's Hebrew word for confusion is "babylon." In Genesis, Babylon is spoken of as Babel, a name that also means "confusion." The city by that name was founded by Nimrod, a rebel against Jehovah. (Genesis 10:8-10) There, men under the leadership of ambitious Nimrod set about building a tower that would soar heavenward in defiance of Jehovah. Jehovah defeated this God-dishonoring project by confusing the uniform language of the builders, so that they could not understand one another while trying to work together. —Genesis 11:1-9.

2 Long afterward, a new city bearing the name Babylon was recorded as existing there at the Euphrates River. (2 Kings 17:24; 1 Chronicles 9:1) In 539 B.C.E. the Babylonian World Power was overthrown by Cyrus the Great, the emperor of Medo-Persia, in fulfillment of Jehovah's prophecy at Isa-

---

1. (a) What does the word "babylon" mean, and who founded the city by that name? (b) What building project did ambitious Nimrod undertake, and with what result?
2. (a) What happened to the world power Babylon in 539 B.C.E., and did that mark the end of the city by that name? (b) What did the ancient city of Babylon not prove to be?

iah 45:1-6. Though Babylon had suffered a significant fall, it was permitted to continue its existence as a city. It is reported as existing even in the latter half of the first century of our Common Era. (1 Peter 5:13) That ancient city, however, did not prove to be "Babylon the Great," which the apostle John wrote about in the book of Revelation chapter 17.

[3] The apocalyptic "Babylon the Great," depicted as an immoral woman who rides "a scarlet-colored wild beast," stands for the world empire of false religion, including all the religions of so-called Christendom.* (Revelation 17:3-5) According to what the apostle John observed about her, this symbolic organization has committed spiritual fornication with all the political rulers of the earth. The world empire of false religion, Babylon the Great, still wields tremendous influence.

"A Friend of the World"—Not of God

[4] However, the position of Babylon the Great is very insecure, and that has especially been the case since the end of World War I. During that conflict, she added to her crimes against the human family. The clergymen of Christendom, who profess to be followers of Jesus Christ, preached the young men onto the battlefields. The late Harry Emerson Fosdick, a prominent Protestant clergyman, supported the war effort but later ad-

* For a detailed identification, see the book *"Babylon the Great Has Fallen!" God's Kingdom Rules!,* pages 468-500, published by the Watchtower Bible and Tract Society of New York, Inc.

3. What is the true identity of Babylon the Great?
4. During World War I, how did Babylon the Great add to her crimes against the human family?

mitted: "Even in our churches we have put the battle flags . . . With one corner of our mouth we have praised the Prince of Peace and with the other we have glorified war." The priests and other clergymen of Christendom offered prayers for the fighting forces at religious gatherings, and they served as chaplains for the army, the navy, and the air force.*

5 Christendom, under the guidance of these religious leaders, has not taken to heart the words of James 4:4: "Adulteresses, do you not know that the friendship with the world is enmity with God? Whoever, therefore, wants to be a friend of the world is constituting himself an enemy of God." Thus Christendom carries on as an enemy of the Most High God down to this very time. Certainly she does not have divine protection, and for this vital reason her very existence remains insecure.

* A detailed discussion of the clergy's support for World War I is given in the book *Preachers Present Arms,* by Ray H. Abrams (New York, 1933). The book states: "The *clerics* gave the war its passionate spiritual significance and drive. . . . The war itself was a holy war to promote the Kingdom of God upon earth. To give one's life for his country was to give it for God and His Kingdom. God and country became synonymous. . . . The Germans and the Allies were alike in this respect. Each side believed it had the monopoly on God . . . Most of the theologians had no difficulty whatsoever in placing Jesus in the very forefront of the thickest fighting leading his troops on to victory. . . . The church thereby became part and parcel of the war system. . . . The [church] leaders lost no time in getting thoroughly organized on a war-time basis. Within twenty-four hours after the declaration of war, the Federal Council of the Churches of Christ in America laid plans for the fullest cooperation. . . . Many of the churches went much further than they were asked. They became recruiting stations for the enlistment of troops." —Pages 53, 57, 59, 63, 74, 80, 82.

5. (a) What words of James 4:4 has Christendom not taken to heart? (b) What must be the divine judgment upon her?

Her political friends are not to be trusted, and the tide in the antireligious direction continues to gain strength. It is not in her behalf that God says: "Do not you men touch my anointed ones." —1 Chronicles 16:22.

"Get Out of Her, My People"

6 To these anointed ones and their associates during this conclusion of the system of things, the divine call rings out urgently: "Get out of her, my people, if you do not want to share with her in her sins." (Revelation 18:4) Yes, get out of the world empire of false religion, Babylon the Great.

7 This call echoes the words of Jeremiah 50:8 and 51:6, 45, which were directed to the remnant of Jews whom Jehovah sentenced to spend 70 years of captivity and exile in the land of Babylonia. Those words began to apply to the Jews who were languishing in Babylonia in 537 B.C.E., after the foretold Cyrus the Great marched his Medo-Persian troops down the nearly dried-up bed of the Euphrates River and into the city of Babylon.

8 In the first year of his rule, Cyrus the Great acted in fulfillment of the prophecy at Isaiah 45: 1-6. Similarly, the one foreshadowed by Emperor Cyrus, but who is far mightier, Jesus Christ, acted according to this prophetic pattern of things. This

6, 7. (a) What urgent call is sounded at Revelation 18:4, and to whom is it directed? (b) When did an earlier but similar call begin to apply to the Jews languishing in ancient Babylon?

8. (a) How did Cyrus the Great fulfill Isaiah 45:1-6? (b) Why did the one foreshadowed by Cyrus the Great need to act according to this prophetic pattern of things?

was at the due time after he had entered in upon his royal reign in heaven at the right hand of Jehovah God, when "the appointed times of the nations" expired in October 1914. (Luke 21:24) During the first world war of 1914-18, the remnant of spiritual Israelites experienced a captivity at the hands of Babylon the Great and her political paramours.

[9] For example, in the United States the latest book to be published by the Watch Tower Society at that time, *The Finished Mystery,* was banned as seditious. The two authors of the book were brought into federal court in Brooklyn, New York, and unjustly sentenced to 20 years of confinement in the federal penitentiary at Atlanta, Georgia. So were the president of the publishing society, the secretary-treasurer, and three others of the headquarters staff. An associate translator was sentenced to half that amount of time in the federal penitentiary.

[10] And so on July 4, 1918, these eight dedicated Christians were put on a train to Atlanta, Georgia, to be deprived of liberty there. Members of the Brooklyn headquarters of the Watch Tower Society then had to take care of matters to the best of their ability. Who was to blame for this situation? The book *Preachers Present Arms* answers: "An analysis of the whole case leads to the conclusion that the churches and the clergy were originally

---

9, 10. (a) What action was taken against eight members of the Society's headquarters staff? (b) What evidence is there that Babylon the Great was behind the movement to stop the work of Jehovah's people?

behind the movement to stamp out the Russellites [Witnesses]. . . . When the news of the twenty-year sentences reached the editors of the religious press, practically every one of these publications, great and small, rejoiced over the event. I have been unable to discover any words of sympathy in any of the orthodox religious journals."—Ray H. Abrams, pages 183, 184.

A Fall—But Not Into Destruction

[11] But the rejoicing in Babylon the Great was not to last for long. In the spring of 1919, Babylon the Great suffered a significant fall, following which there must come certain religious developments before she is totally destroyed. Babylon the Great thought to keep Jehovah's people suppressed and in captivity forever. But in March of 1919 the prison doors were forced open to the eight representatives of the Watch Tower Society, and out they came on bail. Later, they were completely exonerated of all charges.

[12] Gone now was the rejoicing by Babylon the Great! Says the book *Preachers Present Arms* concerning the court's decision to free the Witnesses: "This verdict was greeted with silence in the churches." But great was the joy of Jehovah's people. Their worldwide organization was repaired. At their convention in 1919 at Cedar Point, Ohio, the Society's president roused the thousands in attendance into action by his talk

---

11, 12. (a) What had Babylon the Great intended to do? (b) How did she suffer a significant fall, though not into destruction? (c) What was the effect upon Jehovah's liberated people?

"Announcing the Kingdom." Jehovah's Witnesses were again free, courageously proclaiming God's Kingdom publicly! Babylon the Great had suffered a fall, though not into destruction. The Greater Cyrus, Jesus Christ, had defeated her and had liberated his faithful followers.

13 Thus Babylon the Great was permitted to survive into the postwar era. When the League of Nations was proposed as a world peacekeeping body, the Federal Council of the Churches of Christ in America came out in support of it, publicly announcing that the League of Nations was "the political expression of the Kingdom of God on earth." When the proposed League was finally established, Babylon the Great climbed onto its back and thus began her ride on this symbolic "scarlet-colored wild beast."—Revelation 17:3.

14 When this ineffective peacekeeping agency went into the abyss of inactivity at the outbreak of World War II, Babylon the Great was left without a mount. (Revelation 17:8) But she was right out there with the 57 nations that got embroiled in World War II. Her having to divide her loyalties between the warring factions did not bother her, even as her being divided up into many hundreds of confusing religious sects and denominations has never disturbed her. When the man-made peacekeeping agency, in the form of the United

---

13. When the League of Nations appeared on the scene, what did Babylon the Great do?

14. (a) During World War II, what was the course of action of Babylon the Great? (b) When the man-made peacekeeping agency ascended out of the abyss after World War II, what did Babylon the Great do?

Nations, ascended out of the abyss of inactivity at the close of World War II, Babylon the Great immediately climbed upon its back and started exercising her influence over it.

Political Powers to Turn Against Babylon

15 The whole world of mankind is now about to face an awe-inspiring spectacle. This will be the turning of the political powers against Babylon the Great, with the aim of wiping her out of existence. This may sound heart paralyzing to people who sincerely believe that all religions are good. But the Universal Sovereign, Jehovah God, has determined that Babylon the Great has no place in all the universe and that she has befouled the realm of creation long enough. She must be violently brought down to utter destruction.

16 There are already on hand powerful agencies that God can allow to effect her destruction, namely, the political elements of the world. The God-inspired book of Revelation foretells that Jehovah will turn her lovers against her, and they will strip her naked, exposing her for what she really is—a demonized fraud! And then they will, so to speak, burn her with fire and reduce her to a pile of ashes. They will give her a treatment similar to what she gave to the uncompromising worshipers of the true God.—Revelation 17:15-18; 18:24.

17 This violent antireligious action on the part of

15, 16. (a) Mankind is now face to face with what awe-inspiring spectacle? (b) What has Almighty God determined, in harmony with Revelation 17:15-18?

17. Do the anti-Babylon exploits of the political powers turn them to the worship of Jehovah God, and how do we know?

the political powers does not mean that they will thereafter turn to the worship of Jehovah God. Their fierce anti-Babylon action does not mean that they will now become the friends of God. Otherwise they would not take the later action that the book of Revelation shows that they will take. (Revelation 17:12-14) They may rejoice immensely at the antireligious exploits that Jehovah God has permitted them to accomplish, but they will still continue to be misled by "the god of this system of things," Satan the Devil, the all-out, relentless opposer of Jehovah God.—2 Corinthians 4:4.

18 Babylon the Great will not survive to see the grand climax, the vindication of Jehovah's universal sovereignty by means of the "Prince of Peace," who is now the "Mighty God" at the right hand of the One Almighty and Supreme Deity, Jehovah. —Isaiah 9:6.

19 On the sidelines, under impenetrable divine protection, will be the witnesses of Jehovah. (Isaiah 43:10, 12) Under command from the righteous heavens, they will obediently have got out of Babylon the Great. (Revelation 18:4) Their righteous pleasure will be unbounded at what they witness. They will thereafter forever be witnesses of Jehovah and eternally be able to testify with regard to his vindication of himself over Babylon the Great.—Revelation 19:1-3.

18, 19. (a) Who will not survive to see the vindication of Jehovah's universal sovereignty by means of the "Prince of Peace"? (b) But who will be ever-living witnesses to Jehovah's vindication over Babylon the Great?

Chapter 5

Enlightenment for "the Conclusion of the System of Things"

CONCERNING "the conclusion of the system of things," the "Prince of Peace" said at Matthew 24:38 that there would be "men marrying and women being given in marriage." But during the same period, there begins in heaven the greatest marriage of all. It is the marriage referred to in Jesus' illustration of ten lamp bearers, ten virgins.—Matthew 24:3; 25:1-12.

2 The scene of this marriage is in the Middle East. It takes place late at night, verging onto midnight. The wedding of the bride and her bridegroom is held first and is followed by a procession to the house of feasting. The way is not lighted up by street lamps. Illumination is provided by those sharing in the gala procession, and bystanders can watch the procession go by, wishing the newlyweds happiness.

3 True to their feminine inclination, virgins are

---

1. For this "conclusion of the system of things," what notable marriage did the "Prince of Peace" foretell, and in what parable?

2. (a) At what time of day does this parabolic marriage take place? (b) What follows the wedding, and how is illumination provided?

3, 4. (a) Who interest themselves in the procession that follows, and with what preparations? (b) Fulfillment of this parable adds proof of what fact? (c) We can be happy if we do what?

interested in the wedding. So, along the line of march, ten virgins wait until the wedding procession reaches their location. They desire to brighten the occasion, and for this reason all of them bring along lighted hand lamps, but only five of them have an emergency supply of lighting oil. These five are discreet virgins. The fulfillment of this parable should interest us today, for according to Jesus Christ, it further confirms that we are in the conclusion of this old system.—Matthew 25:13.

4 We can be happy if we are discreet and discern the realization of this marriage of all marriages and its attendant features! Who today are the ones favored with admittance to the feast? Are any of us? Let us see!

5 The illustration that Jesus gave of the ten virgins has to do with "the kingdom of the heavens," the world government for the blessing of all mankind. So Jesus Christ went on to say: "The kingdom of the heavens will become like ten virgins that took their lamps and went out to meet the bridegroom. Five of them were foolish, and five were discreet. For the foolish took their lamps but took no oil with them, whereas the discreet took oil in their receptacles with their lamps. While the bridegroom was delaying, they all nodded and went to sleep."—Matthew 25:1-5.

6 Now whom did those ten virgins illustrate? They illustrated the prospective members of the

---

5. What made a distinction among those composing the ten virgins, and what happened during the bridegroom's delay?
6. (a) Whom did the ten virgins picture? (b) Why is a bride not mentioned in the parable?

bride of the spiritual Bridegroom, Jesus Christ. Doubtless for this reason a bride is not mentioned in Jesus' illustration; merely the bridegroom appears. Thus, there is no confusion regarding the explanation, as if the virgins pictured still another class.

7 The uniting of the prospective members of the bride class to their heavenly Bridegroom in marriage did not take place, as had been expected, at the close of "the appointed times of the nations" in 1914. (Luke 21:24) Logically, to them it appeared as if the Bridegroom had delayed his coming, although his presence in his heavenly Kingdom did take place in 1914. Those mournful years of World War I proved to be like a pitch-black night in the experience of the virgins class.

8 Figuratively speaking, a nodding and going to sleep on the part of the virgins occurred. The public preaching of the good news of Christ's coming reign of a thousand years for the blessing of all mankind practically ceased. From the final year of World War I, a crucial period of judgment set in for those figurative virgins. This was because the reigning King Jesus Christ had come to the spiritual temple. On his arrival there, he started judgment proceedings in order to clean up those appointed to render temple service to Jehovah God. (Malachi 3:1-3) This was the time for his manifes-

---

7. During what period did it seem that the Bridegroom had delayed his coming for the bride, and why?

8. (a) How was it that, figuratively speaking, a nodding and going to sleep on the part of the virgins occurred? (b) For what purpose had the Bridegroom come to the temple, and why did this concern the bride class?

tation when, as the heavenly Bridegroom, he was due to receive to himself in heaven the approved members of the bride class who were then already dead.

[9] In 1919, following the release of eight prominent members of the Watch Tower Bible and Tract Society from unjust imprisonment, it was the due time for the virgins class still alive on earth to be aroused from their sleep of inactivity. The work of worldwide enlightenment lay ahead. It was time for them, with lighted lamps, to meet the Bridegroom, who had come to the spiritual temple. This was so that people out of all nations might stream to "the house of Jehovah" that had been exalted above the tops of the mountains, as it were.—Isaiah 2:1-4.

Putting Their Lamps in Order

[10] The discreet ones of the virgins class had brought along an emergency supply of lighting fuel in their receptacles. They underwent no delay in refilling their lamps. The liquid fuel for enlightenment pictured Jehovah's enlightening Word and his holy spirit. So, what did the oil that was drawn from the receptacles of the discreet virgins picture? The reserve amount of Jehovah's spirit that throws light on his written Word and which the anointed remnant of spirit-begotten disciples of the Bridegroom had in themselves when the postwar work of worldwide enlighten-

9. When did it become the time for the virgins class to be awakened from inactivity, and why?

10. What did the oil that was drawn from the receptacles of the discreet virgins picture?

ment regarding "the kingdom of the heavens" was destined to start.

11 The receptacles pictured the figurative discreet virgins themselves as possessors of the symbolic oil of enlightenment. This does not mean that the virgins class was first then anointed with Jehovah's spirit. No, the virgins do not anoint themselves with his spirit. He does it!—Isaiah 61: 1, 2; Luke 4:16-21.

12 In support of their being assigned to the vast work of world enlightenment regarding "the kingdom of the heavens," the discreet virgins were favored with the fulfillment of Joel 2:28, 29 upon them. This is the way the apostle Peter quotes those verses: "'And in the last days,' God says, 'I shall pour out some of my spirit upon every sort of flesh, and your sons and your daughters will prophesy and your young men will see visions and your old men will dream dreams.'" (Acts 2:17) So from 1919 onward the discreet ones of the figurative virgins class were to take up their means of illumination, their symbolic lamps —themselves. This they did in order to impart enlightenment to all those who were yet in spiritual darkness. Because of the kind of lives that they live under the influence of God's Word and spirit, they become "illuminators in the world." (Philippians 2:15) Thus they took up following in the footsteps of the Bridegroom as he prepared to

---

11. What were the symbolic receptacles in which the oil was contained?

12. (a) What prophecy of Joel was due to be fulfilled upon the discreet virgins? (b) When did the time arrive for them to let enlightenment shine by means of their lamps?

take all the members of the bride class to himself in the heavenly Kingdom after their death on earth.—Matthew 5:14-16.

Consequences of Spiritual Foolishness

[13] What, now, about the foolish ones of the virgins class? Jesus goes on to say: "The foolish said to the discreet, 'Give us some of your oil, because our lamps are about to go out.' The discreet answered with the words, 'Perhaps there may not be quite enough for us and you. Be on your way, instead, to those who sell it and buy for yourselves.'"—Matthew 25:8, 9.

[14] Those refusing to share with the foolish ones were not selfish, just discreet. They were sticking to the carrying out of their original, well-wishing purpose of brightening up the dark surroundings in behalf of the Bridegroom. They were in no way obliged to compromise, to reduce their own amount of Jehovah's holy spirit in order to accommodate those who were spiritually foolish. Such foolish ones had not prepared themselves to enter promptly into the privilege of service opening up to them in 1919.

[15] As the peace period opened up, some of those who were professedly dedicated, baptized associates began to show spiritual foolishness. After

---

13. How did the discreet virgins respond to the request of the foolish virgins?

14. Why were the virgins who refused to share their oil discreet rather than selfish?

15. (a) When the peace period opened up, who among the virgins class began to display tendencies toward spiritual foolishness? (b) Why were the discreet virgins unable to help the spiritually foolish virgins?

the death of the Watch Tower Society's first president, Charles Taze Russell, they did not fully enter into the spirit of developments with the visible instrument of Jehovah God under its new president, J. F. Rutherford. Their hearts were not really in line with the way things were being done. They showed a lack of appreciation for the way Jehovah was dealing with his people. Thus, those who were like discreet virgins could not infuse the real spirit of heartfelt cooperation into these foolish ones who were alienating themselves more and more.

[16] Spiritual foolishness was thus made to surface. How? Through a failure to have the symbolic oil at the momentous time when there was a dire need for spiritual enlightenment as new developments moved forward, showing that the Bridegroom was present. So it was the time to go out to meet him with one's lamp all lighted up brilliantly, figuratively speaking. But instead, those resembling the foolish virgins, whose lamps were going out, parted company with the discreet ones.

[17] What an irreparable loss is incurred when one who professes to be counted among the virgins class misses out on the unrepeatable privilege and opportunity of welcoming the spiritual Bridegroom, Jesus Christ! Such a loss the foolish ones among the modern-day virgins suffer, as is indicated in the further words of Jesus' illustration: "While they were going off to buy, the bridegroom

---

16. How was spiritual foolishness made to surface on the part of the foolish virgins?

17. What irreparable loss do those pictured by the foolish [illegible] suffer, as indicated at Matthew 25:10?

Those resembling the foolish virgins will not get into the wedding feast

arrived, and the virgins that were ready went in with him to the marriage feast; and the door was shut."—Matthew 25:10.

[18] What a tragic experience the modern-day foolish virgins undergo! In this blackest period of all human history, they fail to share in the work of enlightening those who sit in spiritual darkness and in the shadow of death at "the war of the great day of God the Almighty"! (Revelation 16: 14) With no oil in their figurative lamps to brighten their path, they left and had to make their way through midnight darkness. For this reason they are not on time to follow in the footsteps of the Bridegroom in the joyous procession through the door and into the brilliantly lighted marriage feast. They have lost their identification as his followers who are in line for being wedded to him in the heavenly Kingdom. They are not found "ready" at the designated time. What a warning example they furnish!

[19] This painful fact is vividly portrayed in the final part of the illustration given by Jesus Christ, the Bridegroom, particularly for us living in "the conclusion of the system of things." So let us now pursue the matter further! Joy-inspiring enlightenment awaits us for doing so, as we shall see in the next chapter.

---

18. (a) With what privilege do the foolish virgins of this century fail to be associated? (b) Why do the foolish ones prove to be too late for taking part in the marriage procession and for entering into the feast?
19. What experience awaits us for pursuing this matter to its conclusion?

Chapter 6

On the Watch During "the Conclusion of the System of Things"

WE ARE deep into "the conclusion of the system of things," but we "know neither the day nor the hour" when time for life-saving enlightenment will end. That is why Jesus said: "Keep on the watch, therefore, because you know neither the day nor the hour."—Matthew 24:3; 25:13.

2 It would indeed be disappointing to a person if he belatedly arrived at the place for a marriage feast and found the door shut. Yet that is what is destined to befall the vast majority of professed Christians in the near future. The "Prince of Peace" illustrated this by these words: "Afterwards the rest of the virgins also came, saying, 'Sir, sir, open to us!' In answer he said, 'I tell you the truth, I do not know you.'"—Matthew 25: 11, 12.

3 Since 1919 spiritual enlightenment by discreet ones with the aid of the "oil" of Jehovah's Word and holy spirit has been available, but foolish ones try to buy spiritual oil from those in Christendom who claim to sell it. (Matthew 25:9)

---

1. Why do we need to keep on the watch?
2. What disappointing experience is to be avoided?
3. (a) The year 1919 proved to be a time for what? (b) Have Christendom's religionists been able to supply the needed spiritual oil?

The religionists of Christendom, however, do not have the right kind of oil. They have not been able to supply illumination about the presence of Jesus Christ as the heavenly Bridegroom. They expect that when they die they will go to heaven immediately and meet him, without having shared in the work of enlightenment during this "conclusion of the system of things."

[4] On the other hand, there have been those who, like spiritual virgins, have proved to have a reserve of the "oil" of the holy spirit and God's Word for the postwar work of worldwide enlightenment regarding "the kingdom." (Matthew 24:14) Those pictured in Jesus' parable as foolish virgins are not sharing in it by letting the light shine on this good news of international importance. They did not have the "oil" of God's enlightening Word and his holy spirit, and the Bridegroom Judge at the spiritual temple discerned this failing on their part. Their hearts proved not to be with the postwar work that was promptly taken up in 1919 by the Christian virgins who were discreet in discerning both time and work.

[5] In parting company from those who supported Jehovah's visible organization, the foolish ones were failing to participate in the worldwide Kingdom witness. They finally acquired "oil" of religious enlightenment, but it was not the right kind of oil. It would not provide illumination for the

---

4. To this date, what have those pictured by the foolish virgins failed to do, and why?

5. In what do the foolish virgins fail to have a part that is essential to their being united with the Bridegroom King?

right event at the right time. So they are not preaching the Kingdom message and "the day of vengeance on the part of our God." (Isaiah 61:1-3) They are not hailing the Bridegroom King as the anointed remnant of the virgins class is doing.

Effect of the Lamplight at Midnight

6 In the mid-1930's, something significant took place. What occurred suggested that the membership of the spiritual bride of Christ had been filled, that there were on earth enough spirit-begotten disciples of the Bridegroom to make up the full number of his heavenly bride.

7 At that time, in 1935, attention began to be called to another class of sheeplike disciples of Jesus. This was the class that had been called to public attention during the first world war. It was on February 24, 1918, that a lecture on the subject "Millions Now Living May Never Die" was delivered to a curious, possibly doubt-filled, audience. At the 1935 convention of Jehovah's Witnesses in Washington, D.C., something positive was introduced about gathering these millions of Christ's "other sheep" into a unified "flock" under Jesus Christ as the "one shepherd." (John 10:16) The identity of this segment of "other sheep" as foretold in Revelation 7:9-17 was pointed out.

8 The remnant of the "little flock" now came

6, 7. (a) What occurred in the mid-1930's that suggested that there were enough virgins to complete the membership of the bride class? (b) Attention was called to what class that now needed to be gathered?

8. Under what obligation did the discreet virgins come in 1935, unanticipated by them?

under the obligation of starting off the gathering of this "great crowd" of the "other sheep." (Luke 12:32) This was because the number of discreet virgins needed to complete Jesus' bride had now been filled. But such virgins were not taken at once to heaven. They are yet to be admitted into that heavenly festal chamber when they finish their earthly course as integrity-keeping witnesses of their God, Jehovah. Because of their faithful work of enlightenment up to 1935, they were ushered into a special privilege that they had never anticipated before the mid-1930's.

[9] Over a half century has passed since 1935, and during these years the number of the discreet ones of the virgins class has been decreasing. On the other hand, the witness work has expanded to worldwide proportions, yes, to include more than 200 distinct lands. Currently, the virgins class has dropped to about 9,000 in number.

Helpful Companions of the Light Bearers

[10] The anointed remnant of figurative virgins are almost crowded out of the picture by the more than three million Kingdom publishers in over 49,000 congregations of Jehovah's Witnesses all around the globe. How could the tiny number of the anointed remnant take care of the witnessing work in the more than 200 lands where those thousands of congregations are located? They could not.

---

9. Into what number has the remaining ones of the discreet virgins changed to date?

10. In view of the immensity of the work, is the remnant of the discreet virgins able to measure up to the need for workers?

[11] They do, of course, Scripturally serve in the foretold position of "the faithful and discreet slave" whom the Bridegroom Master found faithful on his coming to the temple for judgment. Then it was that the division started to take place between the discreet virgins and the foolish virgins of the figurative virgins class. Those counted as "that evil slave" class do not have the oil of God's enlightening Word and his holy spirit in their receptacles to light up their lamps. Thus they did not have sufficient spiritual illumination to discern the "great crowd" of the "other sheep," already being gathered since 1935 as part of the "one flock."—Matthew 24:45-51.

[12] Since World War II, the fulfillment of Jesus' prophecy for "the conclusion of the system of things" is largely due to the role that the "great crowd" of "other sheep" carry out. The illumination from the lighted lamps of the remnant has brightened the eyes of their hearts, and they have been helped to reflect the light to others yet remaining in the darkness of this world. (Compare Ephesians 1:18.) They have helped millions of inhabitants of this earth to discern the presence of the Bridegroom King as the day of his marriage to the complete bride class nears. They have come to be inseparable companions of the remnant of the bride class.

---

11. (a) The identification of "the faithful and discreet slave" caused what to take place among those professing to be virgins? (b) What are those of the "evil slave" class unable to discern because of lack of sufficient spiritual illumination?
12. Who have become inseparable companions of the remnant of the bride class?

13 Since 1935 the lot of these companions of the remnant of the bride class has been a joyful one. They rejoice not only over the grand privileges into which the remnant has already entered but also over the blessed privileges into which they themselves have been conducted by means of the remnant of the bride class.

14 A wonderful text was opened to the understanding of Jehovah's people at the Washington, D.C., convention in 1935, and it foretold a delightful situation for the "great crowd," the companions of the anointed. See them there, "standing before the throne [of Jehovah God] and before the Lamb, dressed in white robes; and there [are] palm branches in their hands"! Listen to what they are loudly crying out for all the public to hear: "Salvation we owe to our God, who is seated on the throne, and to the Lamb"! (Revelation 7:9, 10) They have already exercised faith in "the Lamb of God that takes away the sin of the world," and through him they have dedicated themselves to Jehovah God and have got baptized in symbol of that dedication. (John 1:29) Why, 840 of them got baptized the day after hearing the explanation of Revelation 7:9-17 on Friday, May 31, 1935.

15 More than three million have done the same since that Washington convention in 1935. Thus

---

13, 14. (a) What delightful situation with respect to the companions of the remnant is figuratively set out in Revelation 7:9, 10? (b) What was the immediate response to the explanation of that prophecy?

15. Since then, how many have been baptized, and how are they pictured in Revelation 7:14-17?

they are pictured as clothed with white robes due to having washed them in the cleansing blood of the Lamb. And they have the prospect of coming out of the great tribulation that is ahead for all the world of mankind, having divine protection clear through that tribulation. (Matthew 24: 21, 22) Therefore, they are dramatized as being at the spiritual temple of Jehovah and there worshiping him with the remnant of the virgins class. —Revelation 7:14-17.

16 Profuse thanks, therefore, to the international, multilingual "great crowd" for the overwhelming part that they have played in the fulfilling of the Bridegroom's prophecy at Matthew 24:14!

"And the Door Was Shut"

17 Exactly when the remnant of the virgins class will have entered into the festal marriage ceremonies, and the door then is shut, is not known. But it is unquestionably nearer than ever before, and time is running out! Appropriately, then, Jesus concluded the parable of the virgins with the cautionary words: "Keep on the watch, therefore, because you know neither the day nor the hour." —Matthew 25:13.

18 For this reason the foolish virgins will be taken off guard. By their parting company with the dis-

---

16. To whom, then, are profuse thanks offered for their part in connection with fulfilling Matthew 24:14?

17. (a) When will the door to the marriage festivities be closed? (b) What is it necessary for the remnant of the virgins class and the "great crowd" of their companions to do now?

18. (a) With whom have the foolish virgins now identified themselves? (b) What part of Jesus' parable are they due to experience shortly?

creet virgins, they have become part of this doomed world and classify themselves with all the other religionists out there in the deepening earth-wide darkness. Thus they are destined to experience what the Bridegroom Jesus Christ portrayed in these words of the parable: "Afterwards the rest of the virgins also came, saying, 'Sir, sir, open to us!' In answer he said, 'I tell you the truth, I do not know you.'"—Matthew 25:10-12.

19 So the door to the feast is not to be opened to those foolish virgins. They well pictured those who during "the conclusion of the system of things" fail to make it into "the kingdom of the heavens." (Matthew 24:3; 25:1) Because of holding on to their chosen form of religion, as indicated by their going to the market to buy other oil, they are classified with Babylon the Great.

20 Consequently, when the symbolic "wild beast," which the religious harlot rides, turns against her with its "ten horns," they will have to share her fate. (Revelation 17:16) When such religionists, pictured by the five foolish virgins, see this beginning of the rejection of Babylonish religion by the powerful forces of the political element, they will turn to the Bridegroom King, claiming that they are of "the kingdom of the heavens" class and deserve to be let into the spiritual marriage festivities with the discreet virgins. Shockingly, the one

---

19. Whom do the foolish virgins therefore picture, and why are they to be classified with Babylon the Great?
20. (a) When the foolish virgins see the "ten horns" of the "wild beast" begin to turn against Babylon the Great, to whom will they appeal and on what claim? (b) Why will they nevertheless experience destruction?

whom they address as "Sir," the Bridegroom Jesus Christ, will refuse to recognize them as deserving of admittance into the heavenly Kingdom. And they have not shared any hope of eternal life on earth along with the "great crowd." So nothing remains for these foolish religionists but destruction with the world empire of false religion, Babylon the Great!

21 What a frightful prospect for them! Being aware of this, the remnant and the multitude of their companions will constantly heed Jesus' advice to "keep on the watch." They will always be filled with God's holy spirit and let the light shine fearlessly to the glory of Jehovah God and Jesus Christ. Rewardingly, joyfulness is their assured portion! And princely positions in the "new earth" await members of the "great crowd," as designated by the wedded Bridegroom King.—Isaiah 32:1; compare Psalm 45:16.

22 So this extended fulfillment of the parable of the ten virgins serves as a confirmation of the fact that we are living in "the conclusion of the system of things." How grateful we can be that we have been enlightened to behold this evidence of the nearness of the marriage of Jesus Christ with his complete bride class! Over this celestial marriage, both heaven and the righteous "new earth" will rejoice with unspeakable joy.—Revelation 19:6-9.

---

21. (a) In view of that frightful prospect, what course do the discreet virgins and their companions pursue? (b) What privileges of service do members of the "great crowd" hope to enjoy?

22. (a) Fulfillment of the parable of the virgins serves as a confirmation of what fact? (b) Who will rejoice over this marriage of the Bridegroom King and his virgin bride?

Chapter 7

Settling Accounts Over the Use of Christ's Funds

WITH one exception, there is no government without economic problems. Most governments are in heavy debt. The one government that is an exception is the now widely proclaimed "kingdom of the heavens." (Matthew 25:1) There are still on earth those prospective members of that heavenly Kingdom who are in the service of that government. During this most critical period of all human history, these servants of "the kingdom of the heavens" are being called to account. They have to settle with the government as to how they have used the valuable things entrusted to them.

2 To illustrate this matter, the foremost representative of that "kingdom of the heavens" long ago related a parable, or an illustration. This should interest us today, for the "Prince of Peace" included it in his long-range prophecy concerning "the sign" that would mark his "presence" in the Kingdom with full authority to rule. (Matthew 24:3) We today are inextricably involved with the consequences that follow the fulfillment of the prophetic parable, since our continued existence,

1. What government is without any economic problems, and who now have to settle accounts with this government?
2. Why should we be very interested in a certain parable as told by the "Prince of Peace"?

our very life, is involved. So here now is the way that the "Prince of Peace" told the parable to his apostles a few days before his sacrificial death on Calvary.

The Parable of the Talents

3 "Keep on the watch, therefore, because you know neither the day nor the hour. For it is just as when a man, about to travel abroad, summoned slaves of his and committed to them his belongings. And to one he gave five talents,* to another two, to still another one, to each one according to his own ability, and he went abroad. Immediately the one that received the five talents went his way and did business with them and gained five more. In the same way the one that received the two gained two more. But the one that received just one went off, and dug in the ground and hid the silver money of his master.

4 "After a long time the master of those slaves came and settled accounts with them. So the one that had received five talents came forward and brought five additional talents, saying, 'Master, you committed five talents to me; see, I gained five talents more.' His master said to him, 'Well done, good and faithful slave! You were faithful over a few things. I will appoint you over many things. Enter into the joy of your master.' Next

---

* A Greek talent of silver weighed 654 ounces troy (20.4 kg).

---

3. How did the slaves who received the talents from the master before his departure handle them during his absence?
4. What did the master say to those slaves who increased the number of the talents?

the one that had received the two talents came forward and said, 'Master, you committed to me two talents; see, I gained two talents more.' His master said to him, 'Well done, good and faithful slave! You were faithful over a few things. I will appoint you over many things. Enter into the joy of your master.'

5 "Finally the one that had received the one talent came forward and said, 'Master, I knew you to be an exacting man, reaping where you did not sow and gathering where you did not winnow. So I grew afraid and went off and hid your talent in the ground. Here you have what is yours.' In reply his master said to him, 'Wicked and sluggish slave, you knew, did you, that I reaped where I did not sow and gathered where I did not winnow? Well, then, you ought to have deposited my silver monies with the bankers, and on my arrival I would be receiving what is mine with interest.

6 "'Therefore take away the talent from him and give it to him that has the ten talents. For to everyone that has, more will be given and he will have abundance; but as for him that does not have, even what he has will be taken away from him. And throw the good-for-nothing slave out into the darkness outside. There is where his weeping and the gnashing of his teeth will be.'" —Matthew 25:13-30.

7 In this parable, what is represented by the talents? Something of high value, not monetarily

---

5, 6. What excuse did the third slave give for hiding the talent, and what did the master do to him?
7. What is represented by the talents?

Those who show the traits of the wicked slave are thrown out of the Master's service and into the darkness

but in a spiritual sense. The talents represent the commission to make disciples of Christ. Along with this commission goes the highly privileged opportunity of acting as ambassadors for Christ, the King, to represent the Kingdom to all the nations of the world.—Ephesians 6:19, 20; 2 Corinthians 5:20.

[8] Beyond all question, we today have reached the culmination of the fulfillment of this prophetic parable! There has descended upon this generation the darkest period of all human history! Indeed, there is a fitting darkness outside the visible part of Jehovah's organization into which the "sluggish" and "good-for-nothing" slave class can be thrown at the order of the Master. Such a "darkness outside" depicts the bedarkened condition of the world of mankind, especially in a religious sense. The world of mankind is not enjoying the light of God's favor and blessing. It is not in the light of the knowledge of the Kingdom of God. It is under "the god of this system of things," who "has blinded the minds of the unbelievers, that the illumination of the glorious good news about the Christ, who is the image of God, might not shine through."—2 Corinthians 4:4.

[9] Today the evidence is overwhelming that the one pictured by the "man," who had at least eight

---

8. (a) Into what darkness has the "sluggish" slave class been cast during this "conclusion of the system of things"? (b) Why is the world of mankind not enjoying the light of God's favor and blessing?

9. (a) In fulfillment of the parable, who is pictured by the "man," and how far did he travel? (b) What evidence is there to indicate his return?

silver talents in his possession, has returned from his travels abroad. That "man" is Christ Jesus. His traveling abroad took him into the presence of the Creator of the sun, moon, and stars of our universe. To mark his return, two wars of world proportions, accompanied now by many other wars of lesser proportions, have bloodied our earth. As predicted, these have been accompanied by famines, pestilences, and earthquakes, and by the increasing of lawlessness and the preaching of "this good news of the kingdom" in all the inhabited earth. This has fulfilled the details of what Jesus said would be "the sign of [his] presence and of the conclusion of the system of things."—Matthew 24:3-15.

10 Although not specifically indicated in Jesus' parable, the man traveling abroad, to be absent for a long time, really made his trip to gain "the kingdom of the heavens," earlier referred to in Matthew 25:1. Despite the outbreak of World War I, Jehovah God, whose kingdom over Israel was overthrown in 607 B.C.E., enthroned the rightful Heir of the Kingdom in 1914 C.E., at the due time for the trampling to be halted. No, the Gentile nations did not see with their natural vision the enthronement of the One whom King David called "my Lord." (Psalm 110:1) They could not do so because the man of the parable, Jesus Christ, had said to his disciples, before traveling abroad: "A little longer and the world will behold me no more."—John 14:19.

---

10. (a) Why did the man travel abroad? (b) Why was it that the world of mankind did not actually see his return?

[11] Since the coming to heavenly Kingdom power by Christ was invisible to human eyes, he had to make apparent his presence in the heavenly Kingdom by the sign that the apostles requested of him three days before his martyrdom. Part of that convincing sign was to be that the man would come back from abroad and take up an accounting with his slaves to whom he had entrusted the highly valuable talents. This being the case, that taking of account of those favored with the use of the talents was due to take place after 1914.

[12] This would mean taking account with those who were heirs of "the kingdom of the heavens." This would signify taking an account with the remnant of that Christian body, which had been begotten by God's spirit from the day of Pentecost of the year 33 C.E. (Acts, chapter 2) There was to be a remnant of these ones on earth during this "conclusion of the system of things" from 1914 onward. These would be the ones upon whom the obligation would fall to take the lead in the fulfillment of Jesus' prophecy for that time: "This good news of the kingdom will be preached in all the inhabited earth for a witness to all the nations; and then the end will come." (Matthew 24:14; Mark 13:10) Upon them rests the responsibility of being faithful to the end, in order to be saved into the Kingdom of the heavens. (Matthew 24:13) With their final salvation in view, the Almighty

---

11. (a) What would be part of the sign to mark his return and presence? (b) When would this take place?

12. (a) Upon whom has devolved the obligation to take the lead in giving the Kingdom witness? (b) Their ultimate salvation depends on what?

God has strengthened them to endure until now, in spite of worldwide persecution. This fact evidences his approval of them!

False Claimants to the Talents

[13] Christendom claims to be honorably entrusted with the talents of the wealthy man in Jesus' parable. But when we take an account of her course of action since 1914, at what judgment do we arrive? This: She has not lived up to her claims. Unfaithful to the man of the parable, she has allied herself with the kingdoms of this world; the politicians of those worldly governments are her paramours. She still backs up the United Nations, the successor of the now-defunct League of Nations.

[14] She does not even correspond to the one-talent slave, who proved to be sluggish and who did not increase the belongings of his master. So in this period since the climax of World War I in 1918, Christendom has definitely been exposed as always having been in the darkness outside the Master's well-lighted house. In the dead of night out there in the world is where, figuratively speaking, her weeping and the gnashing of her teeth have already begun to take place. More of it will yet take place when her political paramours turn upon her and strip her naked as the most reprehensible part of all Babylon the Great, the world empire of false religion.

---

13. (a) Who claims to have received the talents? (b) At what judgment of her do we arrive?
14. Where do we find Christendom today?

"Evil Slave" Class Thrown Out

[15] Those who have actually been part of the spirit-anointed remnant and entrusted with the Kingdom valuables, but who have quit making the effort to increase the interests of the returned Master, have been thrown out of the Master's royal service. (Matthew 24:48-51) No longer do we find the sluggish "evil slave" class preaching "this good news of the kingdom." Rather, they specialize upon their personal salvation instead of the interests of God's Kingdom. They now find themselves in "the darkness outside," where the world of mankind is. Their symbolic talent has been taken away from them and has been given to the class that has shown the willingness to use that talent during the remaining part of this "conclusion of the system of things."

[16] Never was there a time more auspicious for proclaiming the "good news of the kingdom" by employing the "talent," that is, the unusual privilege, the opportunity, of acting as "ambassadors substituting for Christ," the reigning King, and making disciples for him. (2 Corinthians 5:20) And as the end draws on apace, it behooves the "great crowd" of "other sheep" to assist those remaining spirit-begotten ambassadors as they zealously make full use of the valuable "talent" entrusted to them.

---

15. Who have fulfilled the picture of the sluggish slave, and where do they now find themselves?

16. (a) For what use of the figurative talents is this the most auspicious time? (b) What obligation now falls on the "great crowd" of "other sheep"?

Chapter 8

Sharing in "the Joy" of the "Prince of Peace"

IN JESUS' parable of the talents, the man who possessed the eight silver talents did not travel abroad simply for pleasure as on a sight-seeing trip. He had a serious reason for traveling abroad; he desired to secure something valuable. He went abroad, as the parable shows, to gain a certain "joy," along with "many things." (Matthew 25:21) Thus he had to travel a long distance, requiring a long stretch of time, in order to apply to the one who could impart to him that particular joy.

[2] Since the wealthy man in the parable pictures Jesus Christ, the man's traveling abroad for a long trip pictures Jesus going to the one Source of the special joy that he had in view. To whom, then, did he go? Hebrews 12:2 tells us: "We look intently at the Chief Agent and Perfecter of our faith, Jesus. For the joy that was set before him he endured a torture stake, despising shame, and has sat down at the right hand of the throne of God." Yes, indeed, Jehovah God is the Source of that joy. It was to him that Jesus went away, leaving his

---

1. (a) For what reason did a certain man travel abroad? (b) What is implied in Jesus' parable, though not directly stated?

2. (a) In Jesus' case, what did the traveling abroad of the wealthy man picture, and to whom did he go? (b) With what did the Master return?

faithful disciples here on earth entrusted with his "talents." The Master returned with "many things" that he had not had when he committed the eight silver talents to his three slaves. An earlier parable given by Jesus, the parable of the "ten minas," specifies that what he came back with was "kingly power."—Luke 19:12-15.

[3] On being newly installed, a king has reason to be joyful, and so do his loyal subjects. We recall the occasion when the Son of God rode into Jerusalem to fulfill the prophecy of Zechariah 9:9. Concerning the fulfillment of that prophecy, it is written: "Most of the crowd spread their outer garments on the road, while others began cutting down branches from the trees and spreading them on the road. As for the crowds, those going ahead of him and those following kept crying out: 'Save, we pray, the Son of David! Blessed is he that comes in Jehovah's name! Save him, we pray, in the heights above!' Now when he entered into Jerusalem, the whole city was set in commotion, saying: 'Who is this?'"—Matthew 21:4-10; see also Luke 19:36-38.

[4] If, then, it was a joyful occasion when he merely presented himself to Jerusalem's inhabitants as the one anointed with Jehovah's spirit for the kingship, how much more was it the case when he was actually enthroned as King at the close of the Gentile Times in 1914? It was a most joyful occa-

---

3. What kind of time was it when Zechariah 9:9 commenced fulfillment in the first century C.E.?

4. After being enthroned as King, why did Jesus Christ have a special basis for inviting his faithful "slaves" into a joyful condition?

sion for him. Then, indeed, he did enter into a joy never experienced before. On settling accounts, he could therefore say to the disciples whom he judged to be "good and faithful": "You were faithful over a few things. I will appoint you over many things. Enter into the joy of your master." (Matthew 25:21) There was now a new joy in which his approved "slaves" could share. What a reward!

5 In 1919 the anointed disciples of the reigning King, Jesus Christ, did enter into an approved condition, and this was attended with immense joy on their part. Nineteen centuries earlier the apostle Paul wrote to his fellow believers to tell them of their exalted position: "We are therefore ambassadors substituting for Christ." (2 Corinthians 5:20) That was written when Jesus was yet merely the heir apparent with the prospect of receiving "the kingdom of the heavens." (Matthew 25:1) So, then, he needed to sit at God's right hand and to wait there for the day of inauguration. But now, since 1919, the approved remnant have been "ambassadors" sent forth by One actually reigning as King. (Hebrews 10:12, 13) This fact was specially called to the attention of the International Bible Students at the Cedar Point, Ohio, convention in 1922.

6 In 1919 they had already had committed to them the equivalent of the "talents" of the reigning King, Jesus Christ. This had enlarged upon

---

5. (a) The apostle Paul was an 'ambassador' for Christ at what stage of affairs? (b) But today the anointed remnant are "ambassadors" for Christ after what development?
6. The postwar efforts of those who had received the "talents" were directed first to what type of work?

their accountability to their reigning King. From the outset, their postwar efforts were directed to a "harvest" work, the gathering of what was "the wheat" class. (Matthew 13:24-30) Since, as Jesus said, the harvest is "a conclusion of a system of things," the postwar year of 1919 was the due time for this harvesting of the wheatlike "sons of the kingdom," the faithful anointed remnant, to begin.—Matthew 13:37-39.

7 Harvesttime is a joyful time for the reapers, as the Master of the harvest enjoys the occasion with them. (Psalm 126:6) This harvesttime has been greatly enriched by the mounting evidence that God's Kingdom by Jesus Christ was set up in the heavens in 1914 and that Jehovah restored a righteous standing to his dedicated people on earth. As a class, they take up the words of Isaiah 61:10: "Without fail I shall exult in Jehovah. My soul will be joyful in my God. For he has clothed me with the garments of salvation; with the sleeveless coat of righteousness he has enwrapped me."

Gathering "a Great Crowd" of Sharers in "the Joy"

8 Little did the anointed remnant who entered into "the joy" of their Master realize that toward the end of the gathering of the last members of the heirs of the heavenly Kingdom there would be

7. (a) Into what sort of time did the harvesters enter with their Master? (b) Into what condition has Jehovah brought the harvesters, and what prophetic statement do they take up?
8. What joy that the anointed remnant had not anticipated was to be their portion at the end of the gathering of the Kingdom heirs?

another joy, something not anticipated. This was to be the ingathering of an earthly class who would live in the Paradise earth under the Millennial Reign of Jesus Christ. Who else but people from this earthly class would be the proper ones to invite to what would be the first disclosure of information concerned with them?

9 So it was that, in response to the invitation published in *The Watch Tower,** hundreds who were seeking a relationship with Jehovah, along with his name people, attended the general convention of Jehovah's Witnesses in Washington, D.C., May 30 to June 2, 1935. At that convention they were stirred to the depths of their hearts to learn that the "great crowd" forevisioned in Revelation 7:9-17 was to be an earthly class.

10 What a great joy the holding of that convention in Washington, D.C., must have been for the Most High God, Jehovah! What a great joy it must also have been for his Son as the Fine Shepherd who would now start to gather these "other sheep" into the "one flock"!—John 10:16.

11 While being led along and pastured, figuratively speaking, the members of the remnant and the increasing "crowd" of the "other sheep" mingle together peacefully and lovingly. The heart of

---

* Page 2 of the *Watch Tower* issues of April 1 and 15, May 1 and 15, 1935.

---

9. Who were specially invited to attend the Washington, D.C., convention in 1935, and what timely information was there disclosed to them?
10, 11. For whom in heaven should this have proved to be a time of special joy?

their "one shepherd" must now swell with joy at having such a large "flock" near the close of this "conclusion of the system of things."

Envoys of the "Prince of Peace"

12 Those sheeplike ones who make up the "great crowd" now have a huge share in the joy of the Master, Jesus Christ. This is largely due to their having an active share in bringing in the ones needed for completing the "great crowd," for which no number is given in Revelation 7:9.

13 The gathering work in which the "other sheep" are sharing has zoomed to worldwide proportions, far beyond the ability of the diminishing number of the anointed remnant to cope with. Accordingly, it has become increasingly necessary for the growing number of the "other sheep" to have an ever greater share in bringing in still more of the "other sheep" with an earthly hope. Thus the "other sheep" are serving as faithful envoys of the "Prince of Peace." Proverbs 25:13 adds: "Just like the coolness of snow in the day of harvest is the faithful envoy to those sending him, for he restores the very soul of his masters."

14 In the parable of the sheep and the goats, the symbolic sheep are the ones to whom the King Jesus Christ says: "Come, you who have been

---

12, 13. (a) Who has been invited to share with the anointed remnant in the joy of the returned Master, and what is the reason for this? (b) The "great crowd" of "other sheep" serve the interests of the "Prince of Peace" in what capacity?

14. (a) What do the symbolic sheep of Jesus' parable at Matthew 25:31-46 inherit? (b) How has the Kingdom been prepared for them "from the founding of the world"?

The Fine Shepherd's heart must now be filled with joy at having so many "other sheep"

blessed by my Father, inherit the kingdom prepared for you from the founding of the world." (Matthew 25:31-46) They inherit the earthly realm over which the Kingdom of the heavens will rule during the Millennium of Christ's reign. Since the time of faithful Abel, Jehovah has been preparing this realm for the world of redeemable mankind.—Luke 11:50, 51.

15 Wise King Solomon of ancient Israel wrote: "In the multitude of people there is an adornment of a king." (Proverbs 14:28) The royal Master of today, Christ Jesus, who is an official far higher than earthly King Solomon, has just such an "adornment" as regards a "multitude of people."

15, 16. (a) What "adornment" of a king, as mentioned by Solomon, does the Master have today in spite of his rule in the midst of his enemies? (b) In what form does the reigning King have this "adornment" today? (c) What have those making up this "adornment" done?

This is true even now before the start of his rulership of a thousand years, yes, when he is reigning in the midst of his earthly enemies, over whom Satan the Devil is the superhuman invisible king. —Matthew 4:8, 9; Luke 4:5, 6.

[16] Today's "adornment" fit for a high official with the rank of king is now found in the swelling number of his "other sheep" who make up the "great crowd." Jubilantly they are crying out in unison: "Salvation we owe to our God, who is seated on the throne, and to the Lamb." (Revelation 7:9, 10) They already experience salvation from the doomed system of things, of which Satan the Devil is "the god." (2 Corinthians 4:4) They have already, figuratively speaking, "washed their robes . . . in the blood of the Lamb" and made them white so as to appear spotless before Jehovah God, the Judge.—Revelation 7:14.

[17] Yet they look forward to the divinely provided salvation that they will experience at Jehovah's crowning victory in "the war of the great day of God the Almighty" at Har–Magedon. His magnificent victory there will result in the vindication of his universal sovereignty, and they will be earthly eyewitnesses because of being preserved alive through the terrible end of this wicked world. (Revelation 16:14; 2 Peter 3:12) What a precious privilege! What great joy the "Prince of Peace" will then share with the surviving "great crowd" of his loyal "other sheep"!

---

17. (a) To what salvation do the "great crowd" yet look forward? (b) What privilege will they enjoy during the Millennial Reign of the "Prince of Peace"?

Chapter 9

God's Covenant With His "Friend" Already Beneficial to Millions

MORE than 1,950 years ago a true friend of all mankind said: "No one has love greater than this, that someone should surrender his soul in behalf of his friends." (John 15:13) The speaker, Jesus, was a descendant of a man who was called the friend of the most outstanding One in all the universe, Jehovah God. This friendly relationship, lopsided though it might seem, has already begun working out for the benefit of millions.

[2] Who was the man of ancient times who won so much for us because of his friendship with God? He was Abraham, a descendant of the man Shem, who was one of the survivors of the global Flood of Noah's day. Abraham entered into a relationship with God, displaying the qualities of a true friend. Moved by love and faith, Abraham acted in harmony with the will of God, and for this reason the Bible writer James states: "The scripture was fulfilled which says: 'Abraham put faith in Jehovah, and it was counted to him as righteousness,' and he came to be called 'Jehovah's friend.'" —James 2:23.

1, 2. (a) What friendly relationship has already begun working out for the benefit of millions? (b) Why was Abraham able to become God's friend?

[3] That man of faith and action was from the city of Ur of the Chaldeans, and he was the first to be called a Hebrew. (Genesis 14:13) This designation came to be applied to his descendants of the nation of Israel. (Philippians 3:5) In view of his making Abraham his friend, Jehovah God also took him into some of His intimate matters. This is indicated by what is written in Genesis 18:17-19.

[4] That illustrates how highly Jehovah God evaluated the faith and confidence that Abraham put in him, resulting in unquestioning obedience on the part of Abraham. So without embarrassment or apology, Jehovah climaxed his statement to the nation of Israel by saying: "But you, O Israel, are my servant, you, O Jacob, whom I have chosen, the seed of Abraham my friend."—Isaiah 41:8.

The Abrahamic Covenant Goes Into Effect

[5] The extent to which one's bond with a loving friend will lead one is exemplified in the fact that the Sovereign of the universe, Jehovah, made a covenant with this mere man, Abraham. At Genesis 15:18 we read: "On that day Jehovah concluded with Abram [Abraham] a covenant, saying: 'To your seed I will give this land, from the river of Egypt to the great river, the river Euphrates.'"

3, 4. (a) What illustrates how highly Jehovah evaluated the faith and confidence that Abraham put in him? (b) With what words did Jehovah bring his statement in Isaiah 41:8 to a grand climax?

5, 6. (a) What covenant did Jehovah make with his friend Abraham? (b) In the face of what contrary circumstances did God make a promise to his friend concerning a "seed"?

[6] The Euphrates was the river that Abraham and his household crossed to enter the Promised Land. At the time of the crossing, Abraham was childless, although he had then reached the age of 75, and his wife was past the age of childbearing. (Genesis 12:1-5) Yet, in the face of such contrary circumstances, God said to obedient Abraham: "Look up, please, to the heavens and count the stars, if you are possibly able to count them. . . . So your seed will become."—Genesis 15:2-5.

[7] The covenant that Jehovah made with his "friend" we call the Abrahamic covenant. That covenant went into effect in 1943 B.C.E. when Abraham complied with God's covenant requirements and crossed the Euphrates on his way to the Promised Land. In that year Jehovah God came under obligation to bless childless Abraham with "seed." The Law that belonged to the covenant made with the nation of Israel at Mount Sinai came into being 430 years later, in 1513 B.C.E.—Genesis 12:1-7; Exodus 24:3-8.

Law Covenant Added to the Abrahamic Covenant

[8] By that time, Abraham's descendants through his son Isaac had become a free people. The nation of Israel had been delivered from Egypt and had been led to Mount Sinai in Arabia. Through Moses

---

7. (a) What is this covenant called? (b) In what year did it go into effect and with what event in Abraham's life? (c) How many years was that before the Law covenant was made with the nation of Israel?

8. (a) What was the purpose of the Law covenant? (b) Did the Law covenant invalidate the Abrahamic covenant?

as the mediator, they had there been taken into the Law covenant with Jehovah God. Since those Israelites were already the natural descendants of Jehovah's "friend," Abraham, what really was the purpose of such a Law covenant? It was to serve as a protection to Jehovah's chosen people. The Law covenant did not cancel the Abrahamic covenant, even though it did show up the nation of Israel as guilty of transgressions in the light of God's perfect law.—Galatians 3:19-23.

9 Figuratively speaking, the Israelites became the "sons" of that Law covenant. They felt that because they were the natural descendants of Abraham, they automatically became the "seed" by means of which all the nations would bless themselves. Has this proved to be the case? No! Today, almost 3,500 years later, we do see the independent secular Republic of Israel, but it is fighting for its life amid many hostile nations.

10 So one's becoming a proselyte Jew today with the idea of thus becoming part of Abraham's "seed" for the blessing of all the rest of mankind is not the way of Jehovah God. What, then, has taken place?

11 The apostle Paul explains the matter for us, saying: "It is written that Abraham acquired two sons, one by the servant girl [Hagar] and one by the free woman [Sarah]; but the one by the ser-

---

9, 10. (a) How did Abraham's descendants generally feel about the "seed" by means of which all nations would bless themselves? (b) Has their thinking proved to be sound?

11. How did the apostle Paul explain what happened to the natural descendants of Abraham?

vant girl was actually born in the manner of flesh, the other by the free woman through a promise. These things stand as a symbolic drama; for these women mean two covenants, the one from Mount Sinai, which brings forth children for slavery, and which is Hagar. Now this Hagar means Sinai, a mountain in Arabia, and she corresponds with the Jerusalem today, for she is in slavery with her children. But the Jerusalem above is free, and she is our mother."—Galatians 4:22-26.

12 The Jerusalem to which the servant girl Hagar corresponded was earthly, being occupied by fleshly Jews. In the days of Jesus Christ, it was the capital of the nation of Israel and was under the Law covenant. (Matthew 23:37, 38) While the Law covenant mediated by Moses was still in force, natural Israel was the visible part of Jehovah's organization. Thus it could be pictured by a woman, by Hagar the servant girl of Sarah.

True Sons of the Abrahamic Covenant

13 On the other hand, "the Jerusalem above" was Jehovah's invisible heavenly organization. Correspondingly, it could be pictured by a woman, by Sarah, the true wife of Abraham. The Law covenant was not made with this organization, so "the Jerusalem above" was free, like Sarah of old. This is the organization that produces the promised "seed," and that is why the apostle Paul could call it "our mother."

---

12. To whom did the servant girl Hagar correspond?
13. (a) What corresponded to Abraham's wife, Sarah? (b) Why can "the Jerusalem above" be called "free"?

14 Really, then, the Abrahamic covenant applies to her as the symbolic wife of the Greater Abraham, yes, to Jehovah's universal organization up there in the heavens. It follows that the spirit-begotten disciples of Jesus Christ are, like the apostle Paul, the sons, or children, of the Abrahamic covenant. Paul goes on to reason that way, saying:

15 "For it is written: 'Be glad, you barren woman who does not give birth; break out and cry aloud, you woman who does not have childbirth pains; for the children of the desolate woman are more numerous than those of her who has the husband.' Now we, brothers, are children belonging to the promise the same as Isaac was. But just as then the one born in the manner of flesh began persecuting the one born in the manner of spirit, so also now. Nevertheless, what does the Scripture say? 'Drive out the servant girl and her son, for by no means shall the son of the servant girl be an heir with the son of the free woman.' Wherefore, brothers, we are children, not of a servant girl, but of the free woman."—Galatians 4:27-31; Isaiah 54:1.

16 Thus that symbolic drama of ancient times foretold that Jehovah God, the Greater Abraham, would set aside the Law covenant that would be

---

14. Does the Abrahamic covenant apply to "the Jerusalem above," and what can the spirit-begotten disciples of Jesus Christ therefore be called?
15. What did the apostle Paul say at Galatians 4:27-31 with regard to "the children" of the Abrahamic covenant?
16. What did the symbolic drama of ancient times foretell with regard to the Law covenant, this leaving what to remain?

made with Israel at Mount Sinai. In this way the addition (the Law covenant) to the Abrahamic covenant would be subtracted, or taken away, leaving just the Abrahamic covenant with its promise of a "seed" by means of which all the families of the earth would bless themselves.

17 So the added Law covenant was to continue until the promised "seed" arrived, and this proved to be Jesus Christ. By a divine miracle, he became a fleshly descendant of Abraham. He became the principal descendant of that patriarch. He not only was Abraham's fleshly descendant but was the Son of God, and hence a perfect human, one who remained "loyal, guileless, undefiled, separated from the sinners." (Hebrews 7:26) However, his becoming God's Chief Agent for blessing all the families of the earth depended upon the sacrificing of his perfect human life and the applying of the value of this in behalf of all mankind. By such self-sacrifice, he would serve as Jehovah's great High Priest, offering up a sacrifice that met all the divine requirements.

Law Covenant Nailed to Jesus' Torture Stake

18 The benefits of this ransom sacrifice would be presented first in behalf of the Jewish nation, of which Jesus had become a member by his miracu-

---

17. (a) How long was the Law covenant to continue? (b) Why was Jesus Christ the principal descendant of Abraham? (c) Jesus' becoming God's Chief Agent for blessing all the families of the earth depended upon what?

18. (a) To whom were the benefits of the ransom sacrifice to be presented first, and why? (b) What did Jesus become?

lous birth through the virgin Mary. This was vitally necessary, for the Jews were under a double condemnation to death. How so? First, they were the offspring of the sinner Adam, and second, they had, because of their imperfection, become accursed by failing to live up to the Law covenant with God. However, Jesus became a curse for them. By being impaled upon a torture stake till dead, he was able to lift the curse from "the lost sheep of the house of Israel." In 33 C.E., the Law covenant was nailed to Jesus' torture stake, and the Jewish sheepfold under that temporary Law covenant was shut down, abolished.—Matthew 15:24; Galatians 3:10-13; Colossians 2:14.

19 So a new sheepfold had to be opened up to accommodate the spiritual sheep of the resur-

---

19. (a) What new sheepfold had to be opened, and what was it to contain? (b) Those brought into the new sheepfold therefore become what?

The Mosaic Law covenant made at Mount Sinai came to an end when it was nailed to the torture stake with Jesus

rected Fine Shepherd, Jesus Christ. The self-sacrificing Fine Shepherd is also the symbolic door to this new sheepfold. (John 10:7) Those brought into this new sheepfold under the Fine Shepherd become the spirit-begotten sons of the Greater Abraham and thus part of His "seed." (Romans 2:28, 29) True to this fact, during these last days a remnant of that spiritual "seed" has been serving as a blessing to increasing millions of people in more than 200 lands.

Chapter 10

What God Swore to Do for Mankind—Now at Hand!

DOES God swear? Yes, God swears, but he does not use profanity, exploding in anger and losing self-control. His swearing is always in order to reinforce what he declares to be his purpose. It gives added assurance to those who are to be affected. Hence, all mankind does well to give attention to his words at Isaiah 45:23: "By my own self I have sworn—out of my own mouth in righteousness the word has gone forth, so that it will not return—that to me every knee will bend down, every tongue will swear."

2 Today, more than 2,700 years after that prophecy, are we convinced that the prophet's statement at Isaiah 45:24 is true: "Surely in Jehovah there are full righteousness and strength. All those getting heated up against him will come straight to him and be ashamed"? If so, then we can also agree with Isaiah's next words in verse 25: "In Jehovah all the seed of Israel will prove to be right and will boast about themselves."

3 When reading Isaiah 45:25, are we to think of

1, 2. (a) In what sense does God swear, and why? (b) What does God say at Isaiah 45:23? (c) With what statements by the prophet Isaiah should we be able to agree?
3, 4. (a) Why should Isaiah 45:25 not cause us to think of the Republic of Israel? (b) Has there been any failure in the fulfillment of Isaiah 45:23-25, and why do you so answer?

the Republic of Israel? No! Those Israelis do not attribute their conquest to the God of their sacred Hebrew Scriptures. Out of mistaken reverence they even refuse to pronounce his name.

[4] By this, are we arguing that Isaiah 45:23-25 has failed of fulfillment up to this year? No! There has been no failure in the fulfillment of the prophecy at Jehovah's appointed time. With him, failure of his prophecy is an impossibility! Not only is his word by itself reliable and dependable but it is all the more so when Jehovah swears to it, adds his oath, to confirm matters.

God Steps In With an Oath

[5] Concerning this, we read at Hebrews 6:13-18: "For when God made his promise to Abraham, since he could not swear by anyone greater, he swore by himself, saying: 'Assuredly in blessing I will bless you, and in multiplying I will multiply you.' And thus after Abraham had shown patience, he obtained this promise. For men swear by the one greater, and their oath is the end of every dispute, as it is a legal guarantee to them. In this manner God, when he purposed to demonstrate more abundantly to the heirs of the promise the unchangeableness of his counsel, stepped in with an oath, in order that, through two unchangeable things in which it is impossible for God to lie, we who have fled to the refuge may have strong encouragement to lay hold on the hope set before us."

---

5. How does Hebrews 6:13-18 explain God's stepping in with an oath in the promise to Abraham?

[6] Generally, there is a powerful motivation for swearing, for uttering an oath. That is especially true when the swearing is of God's own accord, voluntarily. Such a motivation is furnished in this case wherein Jehovah is reported as swearing, yes, swearing by himself. The oath-bound promise that Jehovah made to Abraham, his "friend," affects all of us today. Jehovah appreciated it when Abraham acted upon the divine invitation and left his native land to go to the land that Jehovah would give to Abraham's descendants as a possession. Jehovah could safely make the name of this "friend" great and could use him for the blessing of others. Jehovah could well say to him: "And I will bless those who bless you, and him that calls down evil upon you I shall curse, and all the families of the ground will certainly bless themselves by means of you." —Genesis 12:3; Isaiah 41:8.

[7] When Abraham's wife Sarah was 90 years old, far past the age of childbearing, God miraculously favored her with bearing to Abraham their beloved son, Isaac, in furtherance of His marvelous promise to Abraham. Abraham proved himself ready and willing to offer up even this precious son as a human sacrifice in obedience to the command of his God, Jehovah. This unique demonstration of faith and obedience so moved Jehovah that he said to his "friend," Abraham:

---

6. (a) What motivation was there for God to swear by himself with regard to his promise to Abraham? (b) How could Jehovah use his "friend"?

7. (a) With what miracle did God favor Abraham when his wife was 90 years of age? (b) How did Abraham demonstrate his faith and obedience in a unique way?

[8] "'By myself I do swear,' is the utterance of Jehovah, 'that by reason of the fact that you have done this thing and you have not withheld your son, your only one, I shall surely bless you and I shall surely multiply your seed like the stars of the heavens and like the grains of sand that are on the seashore; and your seed will take possession of the gate of his enemies. And by means of your seed all nations of the earth will certainly bless themselves due to the fact that you have listened to my voice.'" —Genesis 22:15-18.

[9] This is the first place in the Bible where Jehovah is reported as swearing. Because he could swear by no one greater, he swore by himself, binding his own self to it. In this way he made himself responsible to no one but himself. It must be to his own credit that he carries out his own declaration of purpose.

To What Extent?

[10] Abraham entered the promised land of Canaan nearly 4,000 years ago. So by now, to what extent has that covenant made in 1943 B.C.E. been carried out?

[11] Today, there exists the Republic of Israel in the Middle East. In self-interest, it is a member of

---

8, 9. (a) How did Jehovah respond to this demonstration of Abraham's faith and obedience? (b) To whom did God make himself responsible?
10. About how long ago did God make his covenant with Abraham, and what question therefore arises?
11. (a) What does the Republic of Israel's membership in the UN indicate, and with what consequences? (b) Are the natural descendants of Abraham measuring up to the requirements to be the promised "seed"?

the United Nations. The UN represents the rejection of the Kingdom of Jehovah God through the promised "seed" of Abraham and so will be destroyed in "the war of the great day of God the Almighty," Armageddon. Every member of the UN, including the Republic of Israel, will be blotted out of existence. Unhappily, the fleshly, natural descendants of Abraham are not measuring up to the requirements to be the promised Messianic "seed" by means of which Jehovah God will bless all mankind.—Revelation 16:14-16.

[12] Plainly enough for everybody to note, the promised Messiah does not rule in Middle Eastern, earthly Jerusalem for the fulfillment of the Abrahamic covenant. Unlike his forefather David of old, the Messiah and "Prince of Peace" is not to rule alone. He promised to associate with himself in his rulership his 12 faithful apostles and his other spirit-begotten disciples, to the number of 144,000. (Revelation 7:1-8; 14:1-4) There is yet a remnant of such disciples on earth. What has been done for them in advancing the fulfillment of the Abrahamic covenant to which God swore? One who was a leading prospective associate in that Kingdom, the apostle Paul, wrote at Galatians 3:8: "Now the Scripture, seeing in advance that God would declare people of the nations righteous due to faith, declared the good news beforehand to Abraham, namely: 'By means of you all the nations will be blessed.'"

12, 13. (a) Unlike his forefather David, why is the "Prince of Peace" not to reign alone? (b) Did anointed Christians have to wait until the Kingdom was set up in 1914 to receive the promised blessing, and how do we know?

[13] Christians selected from among the nations did not have to wait until after the setting up of the Kingdom in 1914 to receive the promised blessing, for the apostle Paul went on to say: "Consequently those who adhere to faith are being blessed together with faithful Abraham." (Galatians 3:9) Paul was a Christian and was being blessed, and so were all the other spirit-begotten Christians of his day.* Likewise today, the remnant, composed of spirit-begotten Christians who adhere to faith in the Messiah as the principal "seed" of Abraham for blessing all mankind, is experiencing the promised blessing.

[14] By dedicating themselves to Jehovah and symbolizing this dedication by water baptism and then being begotten by the spirit of God to a spiritual estate, these Christians have become spiritual sons of the Greater Abraham, Jehovah God. They have also become joint heirs with Jesus Christ, the Greater Isaac. (Romans 8:17) They are indeed specially blessed according to the Abrahamic covenant. Jehovah has been carrying out what he swore to do, thereby vindicating himself as a truth-teller, One perfectly able to carry out what he solemnly swore to do in his own name.

[15] Each member of the remnant of spirit-begotten Christians is a Jew in a spiritual sense. As

* Referring to the name "Christians," the *Reference Bible* footnote at Acts 11:26 says: "Hebrew, *Meshi·chi·yim'*, 'Messianists.'"

14. (a) How have the anointed Christians been specially blessed according to the Abrahamic covenant? (b) In what way has this vindicated Jehovah?
15. What does the apostle Paul say that each member of the remnant of spirit-begotten Christians is?

the apostle Paul said: "He is not a Jew who is one on the outside, nor is circumcision that which is on the outside upon the flesh. But he is a Jew who is one on the inside, and his circumcision is that of the heart by spirit, and not by a written code." —Romans 2:28, 29.

16 In this "conclusion of the system of things," those spirit-begotten Christians, who are Jews on the inside with a circumcision of their hearts, make up the Jew class that is foretold at Zechariah 8:23, where it is written: "This is what Jehovah of armies has said, 'It will be in those days that ten men out of all the languages of the nations will take hold, yes, they will actually take hold of the skirt of a man who is a Jew, saying: "We will go with you people, for we have heard that God is with you people."'"

17 The "people" with whom those "ten men" want to go to the worship of Jehovah God is the present-day remnant of those who are spiritual Jews, the class that makes up "the faithful and discreet slave" of Matthew 24:45-47. Since the number ten represents completeness of an earthly kind, the "ten men out of all the languages of the nations" would stand for all the symbolic sheep foretold at Matthew 25:32-46. These are of the "other sheep" class that Jesus said he would bring into associa-

---

16. The spiritual Jews make up what class foretold at Zechariah 8:23?

17. (a) Who are represented by the "ten men" who want to worship Jehovah with the present-day remnant of the spiritual Jews? (b) By associating with the spiritual Jews in the worship of Jehovah, what do members of the "other sheep" now enjoy?

The Bible foretold that people from all nations would come into association with spiritual Israel

tion with the sheeplike remnant to form with them "one flock" in the care of the "one shepherd," himself. (John 10:16) In this way they get a foretaste of the blessings of the Abrahamic covenant by means of the "seed" of the Greater Abraham, Jehovah God. Certainly, then, what God swore to do for all mankind is at hand!

Chapter 11

Earthly Jerusalem in Contrast With Celestial Jerusalem

THOSE today who are Jews according to the flesh are determined that Jerusalem in the Middle East shall endure forever. Even the peoples of Christendom still highly regard that city where Jesus ended his ministry. But does all of this guarantee the continued existence of that city? It has suffered destruction before, in 607 B.C.E. by the Babylonians and in 70 C.E. by the Romans. Would it mean a calamity for all mankind if it again suffered destruction? No, the city is not needed for the blessings of the Abrahamic covenant to flow to mankind. Even of Abraham it is written: "He was awaiting the city having real foundations, the builder and maker of which city is God."—Hebrews 11:10.

[2] The apostle Paul wrote: "But the Jerusalem above is free, and she is our mother." (Galatians 4:26) He there showed that celestial, or heavenly, Jerusalem corresponded to Sarah and was the wifelike organization of the Greater Abraham, Je-

---

1. (a) Would the destruction of Jerusalem be anything new? (b) Why would it not be a calamity for all mankind if Jerusalem again suffered destruction?
2. (a) How does the apostle Paul show that there is a higher Jerusalem? (b) Who is the Husbandly Owner of that Jerusalem, and who are his sons by her?

hovah God. Hence, the sons of "the Jerusalem above" are the spirit-begotten Christians, like Paul.

"Jerusalem Above" Becomes a Royal City

[3] "Jerusalem above" has taken on a royal aspect since "the appointed times of the nations" ended in 1914. (Luke 21:24) From then on, Psalm 97:1 applies: "Jehovah himself has become king! Let the earth be joyful." Likewise Psalm 99:1, 2 applies: "Jehovah himself has become king. . . . Jehovah is great in Zion, and he is high over all the peoples." In 1914 the time came for him to stop the trampling upon the Kingdom in the royal line of David, as represented in the once royal city of Jerusalem. Hence, he enthroned his Son, Jesus Christ, as King at His own right hand in "the Jerusalem above," the celestial Jerusalem, in this way making it a royal city. Jehovah's own kingship is reinforced or enlarged upon by the enthronement of Jesus Christ as King.

[4] So after the birth of the heavenly Kingdom in 1914 and after Satan and his demons were ousted from heaven, it was proper to announce: "Now have come to pass the salvation and the power and the kingdom of our God and the authority of his Christ, because the accuser of our brothers has been hurled down, who accuses them day and night before our God!" (Revelation 12:1-10) "The

---

3. (a) When did Jehovah God himself begin to reign? (b) Where was Jesus Christ enthroned, and what effect did this have on Jehovah's own kingship?
4. By what events has "the Jerusalem above" become a royal city since 1914?

authority of his Christ" was for this One to rule as King in "the Jerusalem above." Truly, she became a royal city in that auspicious year of 1914.

The Daughter of "Jerusalem Above"

[5] More than a quarter of a century after the destruction of Jerusalem by the Roman legions in 70 C.E., the apostle John was given the marvelous visions in the book of Revelation. In Revelation 21:1, 2, John speaks of a "New Jerusalem." It is those who make up this "New Jerusalem" who joyfully welcome the newly installed King who comes in Jehovah's name, just as they are called upon to do in Zechariah 9:9, 10, in these words:

[6] "Be very joyful, O daughter of Zion. Shout in triumph, O daughter of Jerusalem. Look! Your king himself comes to you. He is righteous, yes, saved; humble, and riding upon an ass . . . And I shall certainly cut off the war chariot from Ephraim and the horse from Jerusalem. And the battle bow must be cut off. And he will actually speak peace to the nations; and his rulership will be from sea to sea and from the River to the ends of the earth."

[7] This prophecy had partial fulfillment in the triumphal ride of Jesus Christ into Jerusalem in 33 C.E. Since 1919 it has had its final fulfillment upon the remnant of spiritual Israel. There is no division between the members of that anointed

---

5, 6. (a) In Revelation 21:1, 2, John sees what new symbolic city? (b) By whom is the royal welcome as set forth in Zechariah 9:9, 10 extended, and in what words?
7. By whom has that prophecy been fulfilled during this "conclusion of the system of things," and in what way?

remnant, such as broke out between the tribes of ancient Ephraim and Jerusalem, the capital of the two-tribe kingdom of Judah. By serving in oneness the interests of the Messianic Kingdom for the purpose of carrying out Jesus' prophecy at Matthew 24:14 and Mark 13:10, they continue hailing the triumphant King, Jesus Christ. In unbreakable unity they loyally submit to his kingly rule during this "conclusion of the system of things." —Matthew 24:3.

[8] To their shame, along with Jerusalem of the Republic of Israel, the reputedly Christian nations that make up Christendom do not welcome the victorious King who comes in Jehovah's name. All the same, there are those who are witnesses of the One in whose name he comes, jubilantly serving Him in His temple. (Isaiah 43:10-12) Their spiritual eyes have been opened to see that the Republic of Israel and all the other nations inside and outside the UN are now far along on the march to "the place that is called in Hebrew Har–Magedon." (Revelation 16:16) The war of the Almighty God is near at hand!

[9] The outlook for earthly Jerusalem is tragic, but that of the New Jerusalem is brilliant. In due course, "the ten horns" of the political "wild beast," as well as the "beast" itself, turn to hating the harlot system, Babylon the Great, the world empire of false religion. They will express their violent hatred against religiously revered earthly

8. (a) Who fail to welcome the victorious King? (b) To where and what are such ones marching?
9. How does the future of earthly Jerusalem stand in stark contrast with that of the New Jerusalem?

Jerusalem and will destroy it as if by a conflagration. (Revelation 17:16) But they will absolutely be unable to touch the heavenly New Jerusalem.

[10] The remnant of spirit-begotten Christians who expect to become part of the heavenly New Jerusalem keep on hailing the Bridegroom King, Jesus Christ, together with the "great crowd" of other witnesses of Jehovah. In this loyal course of action, they stand out in sharp contrast with the old Jerusalem. Ever since the founding of the Republic of Israel, the now dominantly Jewish city of Jerusalem follows in the course of the inhabitants of first-century Jerusalem. Under blinding religious influence, she continues to reject Jesus Christ, the One who has the right and the power to rule in the heavenly Kingdom.

[11] True, since the end of the Gentile Times in 1914, the "Prince of Peace" has been ruling in the heavens, unseen to human eyes. Nonetheless, ever since Jerusalem was captured by the British in World War I and the mandate over it was given to Britain by the League of Nations, the good news of the heavenly Kingdom in the hands of the Messianic Son of King David has been "preached in all the inhabited earth for a witness to all the nations," just as Jesus Christ himself foretold.—Matthew 24:14.

---

10. How does earthly Jerusalem pursue a course different from that of spirit-begotten Christians and the "great crowd," their companions?

11, 12. (a) The notable fulfillment of Jesus' prophecy at Matthew 24:14 has been carried out by whom specifically? (b) What does the Society with which they work have in the Republic of Israel today?

[12] This noteworthy fulfillment of the prophecy has been carried out by Jehovah's Witnesses under the supervision of the Watch Tower Bible and Tract Society. This Society even has a branch office in Tel Aviv, from which the activities of Jehovah's Witnesses throughout the territory of Israel are directed. There are also congregations of active witnesses of Jehovah now proclaiming the Kingdom gospel in that land.

[13] Jesus Christ prophesied that after the preaching of "this good news of the kingdom" is fully accomplished, "the end" would come upon this worldly system of things. (Matthew 24:14) So now the end of earthly Jerusalem is in sight. At this time, there seems to be no need for another Jerusalem to be built on the old site, even to receive the onetime king of Jerusalem, David, by a resurrection from the dead under the Millennial Kingdom of his royal descendant, Jesus Christ. (John 5:28, 29) Nonetheless, David will likely be brought back to the area in which he formerly served Jehovah God.

A Time for Rejoicing

[14] New Jerusalem is associated with the glorious new system of things. Says the apostle John: "I saw a new heaven and a new earth; for the former heaven and the former earth had passed away, and

---

13. (a) What comes after the preaching of the good news of God's Kingdom is fully accomplished? (b) Will there ever be a need for another earthly Jerusalem, even to receive David back in the resurrection?

14, 15. (a) How does the apostle John describe the glorious New Jerusalem and its descent from heaven for the blessing of mankind? (b) Why is ours a time for rejoicing, and what occasion for universal joy approaches?

In the new system of things, New Jerusalem will bless all mankind

the sea is no more. I saw also the holy city, New Jerusalem, coming down out of heaven from God and prepared as a bride adorned for her husband. With that I heard a loud voice from the throne say: 'Look! The tent of God is with mankind, and he will reside with them, and they will be his peoples. And God himself will be with them.'" (Revelation 21:1-3) Thus, New Jerusalem is to be a blessing to all humankind.

[15] This makes ours a time for rejoicing. To add to all this rejoicing, an occasion of universal interest and for universal joy approaches. It is the marriage of the numerically complete bride class, the New Jerusalem, to Jesus Christ the King. As it is written in Revelation 19:6-9: “And I [the apostle John] heard what was as a voice of a great crowd and as a sound of many waters and as a sound of heavy thunders. They said: ‘Praise Jah, you people, because Jehovah our God, the Almighty, has begun to rule as king. Let us rejoice and be overjoyed, and let us give him the glory, because the marriage of the Lamb [Jesus Christ] has arrived and his wife has prepared herself. Yes, it has been granted to her to be arrayed in bright, clean, fine linen, for the fine linen stands for the righteous acts of the holy ones.’ And he tells me: ‘Write: Happy are those invited to the evening meal of the Lamb’s marriage.’”

[16] This union with the Lamb Jesus Christ in marriage will mean unspeakable joy for the figurative New Jerusalem in heaven. Through it she will become “a joyful mother of sons.” (Psalm 113:9) Yes, she will become the heavenly mother to all humans, living and dead, whom her loving husband redeemed by his perfect human sacrifice 19 centuries ago. In full harmony with Jehovah’s Abrahamic covenant of thousands of years ago, the New Jerusalem will prove to be a blessing to all the families of the earth.

---

16. (a) By her heavenly marriage to the Lamb, the New Jerusalem becomes a mother to whom? (b) The New Jerusalem will prove to be a blessing in full harmony with what?

Chapter 12

God's New Covenant Nears Its Accomplishment

WHAT would we do if God did not hold true to his covenant regarding the day and that regarding the night? Instead of having an alternating of day and night, our earth would be illuminated by continual light or shrouded in continual darkness. (Genesis 1:1, 2, 14-19) But God loyally sticks to his covenants. So we can be absolutely certain that the moon, the sun, and the galaxies of the heavens will never be destroyed; neither will our planet Earth.

2 Speaking of his covenant of the day and that of the night, God said to the Jews under the kingdom of the royal house of David: "If you people could break my covenant of the day and my covenant of the night, even in order for day and night not to occur in their time, likewise could my own covenant be broken with David my servant so that he should not come to have a son ruling as king upon his throne."—Jeremiah 33:20, 21.

3 In those words we have an indirect proof that our earth, together with the sun and the moon, will

---

1. (a) What would happen to our earth if God did not hold to his covenant regarding the day and that regarding the night? (b) Since God loyally sticks to his covenants, of what may we be certain?
2. What did Jehovah tell the Jews in connection with his covenant of the day and that of the night?
3. What do these words indicate regarding his covenant with David for an everlasting Kingdom?

remain forever. (Ecclesiastes 1:4) Our earth will ever be occupied by human residents, for them to enjoy the beauties of the day and of the night under the covenant-keeping God, man's Creator. And just as Jehovah has held firm to his covenant of the day and that of the night, so he has kept loyal to his covenant with ancient King David for an everlasting Kingdom in David's family line. This is true even though the seat of the Kingdom has had to be transferred from the earth to the invisible heavens. —Psalm 110:1-3.

[4] God's covenant for an everlasting Kingdom in the line of descent from David is associated with another covenant, "the new covenant." This covenant that was to replace an old covenant was mentioned by Jesus. This was after he had celebrated the Jewish Passover with his faithful disciples on the night of Nisan 14 in 33 C.E. He set up what came to be called "the Lord's evening meal." He knew that, on that same Passover day, he would shed his blood in sacrifice. In view of that, he took a cup of red wine, but before passing it to his faithful apostles, he said: "This cup means the new covenant by virtue of my blood."—Luke 22:20; 1 Corinthians 11:20, 23-26.

[5] Like the old covenant, the new covenant is made with a nation but not with any of the nations of Christendom. Although the promise of the new covenant was made by means of the prophet Jere-

---

4. (a) God's covenant with David for an everlasting Kingdom is associated with what other covenant? (b) What did Jesus Christ say regarding it, and under what circumstances?

5. To whom was God's promise of a new covenant made, and does the Republic of Israel claim to be in this covenant?

miah to the nation of Israel more than 2,500 years ago, the Republic of Israel of today does not claim to be in the new covenant. Instead, the Republic of Israel became a member of the UN.

6 Why did God want a new covenant? Jeremiah 31:31-34 explains: "'Look! There are days coming,' is the utterance of Jehovah, 'and I will conclude with the house of Israel and with the house of Judah a new covenant; not one like the covenant that I concluded with their forefathers in the day of my taking hold of their hand to bring them forth out of the land of Egypt, "which covenant of mine they themselves broke, although I myself had husbandly ownership of them," is the utterance of Jehovah.' 'For this is the covenant that I shall conclude with the house of Israel after those days,' is the utterance of Jehovah. 'I will put my law within them, and in their heart I shall write it. And I will become their God, and they themselves will become my people. And they will no more teach each one his companion and each one his brother, saying, "Know Jehovah!" for they will all of them know me, from the least one of them even to the greatest one of them,' is the utterance of Jehovah. 'For I shall forgive their error, and their sin I shall remember no more.'"

A Better Covenant With a Better Mediator

7 The new covenant is not a mere renewal of the earlier covenant that the Israelites broke. No,

---

6. According to Jeremiah chapter 31, why did God see the need to make a new covenant, and in what would it result?
7. Is the new covenant a renewal of the covenant that the Israelites broke, and why is it better than the Law covenant?

indeed! For the apostle Paul writes to the Christians at Rome, saying: "You are not under law but under undeserved kindness." (Romans 6:14) It is really a *new* covenant, and it was to be expected that it would be a better one, for the Almighty God Jehovah is able to improve matters with regard to those whom he admits into the new covenant. For one thing, he raised up a better mediator, or go-between, in establishing the new covenant. This Mediator was no imperfect, sin-infected man like the prophet Moses.

[8] The Law covenant mediated by means of the prophet Moses was good in itself. However, that covenant provided for the sacrifice of animals whose blood could never wash away human sins. So for Jehovah God to set up a better covenant, there would have to be a better mediator with a better sacrifice. This all-necessary Mediator proved to be Jesus Christ. Pointing out the superiority of this Mediator as compared to the prophet Moses, the Bible gives us the following explanation: "But now Jesus has obtained a more excellent public service, so that he is also the mediator of a correspondingly better covenant, which has been legally established upon better promises. . . . In his saying 'a new covenant' he has made the former one obsolete."—Hebrews 8:6, 13.

---

8. (a) What does the new covenant have that makes it better than the Law covenant? (b) Who is the Mediator of the better new covenant? (c) What does Hebrews 8:6, 13 say about the new covenant and the superiority of its Mediator, and with what effect on the former covenant?

"Obsolete" Old Covenant Replaced

[9] That "obsolete," or out-of-date, covenant passed away 50 days after the resurrection of the Mediator of the new covenant. This took place on the day of Pentecost. On the morning of that day, the antitype of the Jewish Feast of Ingathering began to take place. How? Well, 120 faithful disciples of the Mediator of the new covenant gathered together in an upper room in Jerusalem and received the promised holy spirit, in fulfillment of the prophecy of Joel 2:28-32. It verified the start of the new covenant by furnishing audible and visible proof to all observers.

[10] When Jesus came up out of the waters of baptism and holy spirit was poured down upon him, the spirit was miraculously symbolized by the image of a dove hovering above his head. But in the case of the 120 Hebrew disciples on the day of Pentecost, how was their being anointed with holy spirit made manifest? By the appearing of tongues as if of fire above their heads and by their being gifted with the ability to proclaim God's Word in foreign languages that they had never learned.—Matthew 3:16; Acts 2:1-36.

[11] It ought to be evident to Jews and their rabbis that the Mosaic Law covenant is no longer in oper-

---

9. (a) On what day did the old covenant pass away? (b) What took place on that morning, and in verification of what?
10. On that day of Pentecost, how was it made manifest that Jesus' disciples had been anointed with holy spirit?
11. (a) What ought to be evident to Jews, and why? (b) How do we know that Jews are not saying to one another, "Know Jehovah!" and what happiness do they not have?

ation. Since the destruction of Jerusalem by the Roman legions in 70 C.E., they have not had a temple. At that time, their genealogical records were lost or destroyed. Thus today they do not know who belongs to the tribe of Levi and who is a descendant of Aaron so as to serve in the capacity of high priest for the Jewish nation. Instead of saying to one another, "Know Jehovah!" they consider the pronouncing of the divine name to be a sacrilege. So they do not share the happiness of Jehovah's Witnesses over the fact that the "obsolete" old covenant has been replaced by the new covenant.

"An Everlasting Covenant"

12 In stark contrast with the Jewish situation of today, Jehovah's Witnesses have an active, officiating High Priest at God's right hand in the heavens. He is the Mediator of the new covenant, a mediator far greater than Moses. From the heart, these witnesses of Jehovah can join the writer's prayer at Hebrews 13:20, 21: "Now may the God of peace, who brought up from the dead the great shepherd of the sheep with the blood of an everlasting covenant, our Lord Jesus, equip you with every good thing to do his will." Since that "great shepherd" laid down his human life for "the sheep," he could be resurrected from the dead in an immortal, bloodless spirit body but with the value of the blood of the new covenant that is faithfully kept and that is everlasting in its good effects.

---

12. (a) In what prayer can Jehovah's Witnesses join from the heart? (b) With what was Jesus resurrected from the dead?

[13] The sacrificial death of the Mediator of the new covenant, Jesus Christ, is remembered every year by Jehovah's Witnesses on the anniversary of "the Lord's evening meal." The unleavened bread partaken of by those in the new covenant during that "evening meal" symbolizes the perfect flesh of the Mediator, and the wine symbolizes the pure, uncontaminated blood that, according to the Scriptures, contained the very life value of the Mediator. —1 Corinthians 11:20-26; Leviticus 17:11.

[14] When those in the new covenant partake of the Memorial cup of wine at "the Lord's evening meal," it is only in a figurative way that they are drinking blood, that of the Mediator of the new covenant. It is also in a symbolic way that they eat his flesh when they partake of the Memorial loaf of unleavened bread. By doing this, symbolically speaking, they demonstrate their faith in the ransom sacrifice of the Son of God, the Redeemer of all mankind.

[15] The new covenant, now more than 1,950 years old, is nearing the accomplishment of its purpose. Already it has lasted centuries longer than the Mosaic Law covenant. Being based upon better promises and a better sacrifice with a better Mediator, it has indeed proved to be a better covenant.

---

13. (a) How is the death of the Mediator of the new covenant remembered every year by Jehovah's Witnesses? (b) What do the emblems symbolize?
14. When those in the new covenant partake of the Memorial emblems, what are they doing, symbolically speaking?
15. (a) How long has the new covenant already lasted, and how has it indeed proved to be a better covenant? (b) Why can the new covenant be referred to as "an everlasting covenant"?

The new covenant mediated by Jesus is far superior to the old covenant mediated by Moses

Because of not needing to be superseded or replaced by a new and better covenant, the successful new covenant is referred to as "an everlasting covenant."—Hebrews 13:20.

16 Thanks to the Almighty God, Jehovah, that he has raised up a Mediator better than Moses, by means of whom He could legally take the Mosaic Law covenant out of the way by nailing it to the torture stake and provide the blood of the everlasting new covenant!

---

16. For what should we be thankful to Jehovah God?

Chapter 13

The "Prince of Peace" Turns to Those Outside the New Covenant

NATURAL Jews today, those who are the fleshly descendants of the patriarch Abraham, cannot deny that the old Mosaic Law covenant was to be superseded by a new and better covenant. They cannot expunge from their manuscripts of the Hebrew Scriptures the words of God at Jeremiah 31:31: "'Look! There are days coming,' is the utterance of Jehovah, 'and I will conclude with the house of Israel and with the house of Judah a new covenant.'"

[2] Who the mediator of that new covenant would be was not foretold by Jeremiah. But on the night of Nisan 14, 33 C.E., when Jesus Christ handed the cup with the Passover wine to his disciples, he showed that he was to be that Mediator. (Luke 22:20) At Hebrews 7:22 we are told that he is the "pledge," surety, or guarantee, of such a new and "better covenant."

[3] By his sacrifice in behalf of the new covenant,

---

1. Why cannot the Jews of today deny that the Mosaic covenant made with their forefathers was to come to an end?
2. How was the question of who would be the Mediator of the new covenant finally disclosed?
3. What other office toward God does Jesus Christ hold, and was it by line of descent?

Jesus became Jehovah's High Priest. He did not become such by natural descent from Aaron, the first high priest of Israel. He was sworn into the office of High Priest by the oath of the Most High God, Jehovah, the Priest-Maker. The words of Psalm 110:4 apply to Jesus: "Jehovah has sworn (and he will feel no regret): 'You are a priest to time indefinite according to the manner of Melchizedek!'"—Hebrews 7:20, 21.

[4] With the exception of a small remnant, the nation of natural Israel rejected Jesus Christ as the Mediator of the new covenant. Thus "the house of Israel" with which God made the foretold new covenant proved to be a spiritual Israel, "the Israel of God." (Galatians 6:16) That spiritual Israel was brought to birth on the day of Pentecost, 33 C.E. Being spiritual, it could take into its citizenship believing non-Jews, or Gentiles. (Acts 15: 14) Peter addressed it as "a chosen race, a royal priesthood, a holy nation, a people for special possession." (1 Peter 2:9) This "holy nation" is composed of the spiritual sons of the Greater Abraham, Jehovah, the Maker and Fulfiller of the Abrahamic covenant. Hence, they are at the same time the "sons" of Jehovah's wifelike heavenly organization, prefigured by Sarah, the wife of Abraham. Unavoidably, the new covenant of the Greater Abraham takes into account that heavenly organization as the mother of the promised "seed," prefigured by Isaac.

---

4. (a) With what sort of "Israel" did Jehovah make the promised new covenant, and why? (b) Those taken into the new covenant become the sons of what parents?

"Other Sheep" Included in One Flock

[5] That new covenant needed active ministers down here on earth, and the members of the anointed remnant have served as the adequately qualified "ministers of a new covenant" that has replaced the old Mosaic Law covenant. (2 Corinthians 3:6) They are not clerical ministers inside the hundreds of religious sects of Christendom, the outstanding part of modern-day Babylon the Great. They have heeded the commanding call of Revelation 18:4 and have come out of that world empire of false religion.

[6] The number of the ministers of that new covenant was to be limited to 144,000. (Revelation 7:1-8; 14:1-5) So the time was bound to come when the Fine Shepherd would turn his attention beyond the ministers of the new covenant. Jehovah's Prime Minister foresaw this and referred to this when he said, at John 10:16, that he had "other sheep," which were not of the "little flock" of 144,000.—Luke 12:32.

[7] While the "other sheep" would not be of the "little flock," they would be ministers of God, too, but not ministers of the new covenant. And the fact that those "other sheep" would become "one flock" with the remnant of those "ministers of a

---

5. What did the new covenant require down here on earth?

6. (a) The number of the ministers of the new covenant is limited to how many? (b) How do we know that the Fine Shepherd would turn his attention to those outside the new covenant?

7. (a) Why are members of the "other sheep" class not ministers of the new covenant? (b) How has the remnant of those in the new covenant already become a blessing to the families and nations of the earth?

new covenant" would indicate something grand. What? This: Before being glorified in the heavenly Kingdom, the remnant would personally associate with the "other sheep" on earth. In this way the remnant of the spiritual seed of Abraham would begin to be a blessing to all the families and nations before "the war of the great day of God the Almighty" at Armageddon and before the start of the Millennium.—Galatians 3:29; Revelation 16: 14, 16.

8 This has actually proved to be the case, particularly since 1935. Since then, millions of those "other sheep" have associated with the tens of thousands of congregations of Jehovah's Witnesses around the globe and have dedicated themselves to the Supreme Shepherd, Jehovah God. They have thus been admitted into the "one flock" of the Fine Shepherd, Jesus Christ.

9 Did the fact that the Mediator of the new covenant was, from then on, widening out his attention to include also the "other sheep" mean that the ministry of the new covenant ended in 1935? No, for there is a remnant of ministers of the new covenant yet on earth, and they still have to finish that ministry.

10 Today, both the remnant of the "little flock"

---

8. When did the Fine Shepherd turn his attention to those outside the new covenant, and what preliminary step have these "other sheep" taken?

9. Did the widening out of the attention of the Mediator of the new covenant mean that the ministry of the new covenant had ended on earth?

10. Who today are benefiting from the ministry of the new covenant as rendered by the eight writers of the Christian Greek Scriptures?

and the increasing "great crowd" of the Fine Shepherd's "other sheep" are benefiting from the ministry of others who went before them, such as the apostle Paul. In carrying out his ministry of the new covenant faithfully until his death in Rome some time before Jerusalem was destroyed in 70 C.E., Paul was inspired to write 14 of the 27 books of the Christian Greek Scriptures. How thankful the anointed remnant and the "great crowd" of the "other sheep" can be that faithful men of the first century, such as the apostle Paul and the seven other writers of the Christian Greek Scriptures, carried out their ministry of the new covenant to the finish of their earthly lives! And in our time, millions of the "other sheep" are already benefiting from the ministry of the new covenant, as rendered by the anointed remnant under the Mediator, Jesus Christ. The "Prince of Peace" has now turned his attention to these dear "other sheep," whose numbers have grown rapidly.

11 However, time must now be running out! The new covenant has already been in effect for 1,953 years, 407 years longer than the Mosaic Law covenant that it replaced, and the number of ministers of the new covenant is diminishing as members pass off the earthly scene in death. But today's remnant of those ministers continue to serve as "the faithful and discreet slave" whom the Master, Jesus Christ, has appointed "over all his belongings."—Matthew 24:45-47.

---

11. (a) How long has the new covenant been in effect, and what does this indicate? (b) The remnant of the ministers of the new covenant serve in what capacity today?

Millions of "other sheep" have come into Jehovah's visible organization in these last days

Extending the Invitation: "Come!"

[12] How loving is the service rendered by those ministers of the new covenant! For instance, in Revelation 22:17 we read: "The spirit and the bride keep on saying: 'Come!' And let anyone hearing say: 'Come!' And let anyone thirsting come; let anyone that wishes take life's water free." The "bride" class, along with Jehovah's active force, or spirit, is extending that invitation to

---

12. According to Revelation 22:17, what invitation is the "bride" class extending, and to whom?

those who are outside the new covenant. The invitation is extended, not to those now dead in the memorial tombs who are to be blessed with a resurrection from the dead, but to people now living, who are in danger of destruction at Armageddon but who have hearing ears.

[13] Not in vain has this loving invitation been extended worldwide especially since 1935. Over three million have already responded to the gracious invitation to come and drink. As those who have appreciatively heard, they are obediently saying to still many other millions athirst for endless life on a paradise earth, "Come!" But the time for extending this gracious invitation to the "other sheep" is limited. After more than a half century of being extended, the time remaining for it should now be very short, as God's war at Armageddon looms ominously over "this generation" of mankind.—Matthew 24:34.

[14] So, now, thanks to Jehovah that he has provided the capable Mediator who is successfully accomplishing the purpose of the new covenant in producing a people, 144,000 strong, for His name! Praise, too, to Jehovah that his Mediator as a Fine Shepherd is already bringing increasing millions of "other sheep" into the "one flock," where they have already entered into the early benefits flowing to mankind from the new covenant!

---

13. (a) Has the invitation extended by the "bride" class been in vain? Explain. (b) What are those who have already accepted the invitation doing in obedience to Revelation 22:17? (c) What must be the case with regard to the time left for extending the invitation?
14. For what should we be giving Jehovah thanks and praise?

Chapter 14

After the New Covenant —The Millennial Kingdom

MILLIONS of people all around the earth have already received grand benefits from the operation of the new covenant, even though they are not in it. They are like the non-Israelite residents who lived in Israel during the days when the Mosaic Law covenant was still in force. (Exodus 20:10) How has this been the case with such increasing millions of beneficiaries who are associated with the remnant of spiritual Israelites today?

2 In the prophecy of Jeremiah 31:31-34, the One laying down the terms of the new covenant said: "I will put my law within them, and in their heart I shall write it. And I will become their God, and they themselves will become my people."

3 In the case of the Law covenant, Jehovah God, by means of the prophet Moses as mediator, gave to natural Israel "the handwritten document . . . , which consisted of decrees." (Colossians 2:14) What, though, about the law of the new covenant?

1, 2. (a) With whom may the millions of beneficiaries of the operation of the new covenant be compared today? (b) What did the terms of the new covenant say?

3. (a) In what form was the law of the old Mosaic covenant given to Israel? (b) Before the Christian Greek Scriptures began to be written, where did God have the laws of the new covenant written?

Its Mediator was not to inscribe it on stone, or to write it in a manuscript. Its Mediator left behind no writings of his own. We ascertain what is the law of the new covenant from the inspired Christian Greek Scriptures. (2 Timothy 3:16) But even before those Greek Scriptures began to be written, from about 41 C.E., Jehovah God began writing his law of the new covenant. When? On the day of Pentecost, 33 C.E. Where? Exactly where he had long before promised to write it: "I will put my laws in their mind, and in their hearts I shall write them."—Hebrews 8:10.

4 Being inscribed upon the heart, those laws would be less likely to cease being loved by those who obeyed them. If those laws were put "in their mind," they would be less likely to forget them. Hence, the keepers of those laws say, in the words of Psalm 119:97: "How I do love your law! All day long it is my concern." From their most inward being, they set their affections upon Jehovah's laws as given through his Mediator, Jesus Christ. Thus, with the right motivation, they determine to keep those precious laws. This applies both to the "little flock" *in* the new covenant and to the "great crowd" of "other sheep" who are, not in the new covenant, but *under* it.—Compare 1 John 5:3; John 14:15.

Kingdom Issue to the Fore!

5 Keepers of the laws of the new covenant dare

---

4. God's writing his laws upon the heart and putting them in the mind of his servants would have what good effects?
5. What did the Mediator of the new covenant foretell at Matthew 24:12-14?

not succumb to what the Mediator, Jesus Christ, foretold as part of "the sign . . . of the conclusion of the system of things": "Because of the increasing of lawlessness the love of the greater number will cool off. But he that has endured to the end is the one that will be saved. And this good news of the kingdom will be preached in all the inhabited earth for a witness to all the nations."—Matthew 24:3, 12-14.

6 This last statement concerning an earth-wide witness to the Kingdom was not a mere prediction. It was a directive for his disciples living in "the conclusion of the system of things." It was a guide for their correct course of action down to the complete end of a system of things that is loveless and ridden with lawlessness in general, not merely with disrespect for God's law. Who today prove to be true Christians, taking those words of Jesus Christ as a directive to them? The historical facts that have multiplied since 1919 truthfully answer, "Jehovah's Witnesses"! Their Bible educational campaign regarding the Kingdom is the greatest on record, and they have shown endurance in it during the past 67 years. Each year now, it grows in scope and power.

7 Satan the Devil tried to prevent this phenomenal Bible educational campaign by having the small remnant of spiritual Israelites wiped out

---

6. (a) Was Matthew 24:14 a mere prophecy? (b) Who have taken it as more than prophetic, and what may be said concerning their endurance?

7, 8. (a) During World War I, what did Satan try to do to those in the new covenant? (b) In the postwar period, how did the Kingdom issue leap to the fore?

during World War I. He failed! Promptly, after their revival from a deathlike state in the summer of 1919, they held their first postwar convention in Cedar Point, Ohio, in September of that year. At the second Cedar Point convention in September 1922, the Kingdom issue leaped to the fore. On the fourth day of that convention, entitled "The Day," the president of the Watch Tower Society brought his thrilling discourse to a grand climax by exclaiming:

[8] "Then back to the field, O ye sons of the Most High God! Gird on your armor! Be sober, be vigilant, be active, be brave. Be faithful and true witnesses for the Lord. Go forward in the fight until every vestige of Babylon lies desolate. Herald the message far and wide. The world must know that Jehovah is God and that Jesus Christ is King of kings and Lord of lords. This is the day of all days. Behold, the King reigns! You are his publicity agents. Therefore advertise, advertise, advertise the King and his Kingdom."

Getting to Know Jehovah More Discerningly

[9] It has now been more than 70 years since Christ was enthroned in Kingdom power in 1914. Since then, the evidence respecting God's righteous government has increased tremendously. The people of the world of mankind have to take their stand regarding the Kingdom issue, either for the Kingdom or against it. And those taking

---

9. (a) Because of the increase of the evidence respecting that righteous government, people have to take what stand? (b) Those taking a favorable stand are being given what knowledge?

their stand for that divine government are having fulfilled toward them these vital words of the new covenant: "They will no more teach each one his companion and each one his brother, saying, 'Know Jehovah!' for they will all of them know me, from the least one of them even to the greatest one of them."—Jeremiah 31:34.

[10] In 1935 the remnant of spiritual Israelites began welcoming the "other sheep" of the Fine Shepherd into active association with them in "one flock" under Jesus Christ, all of them being Jehovah's Witnesses. Then those "other sheep," who began building up to be "a great crowd" without any foreordained number, undertook, along with the spirit-begotten remnant, to "observe the commandments of God" and to do "the work of bearing witness to Jesus." (Revelation 7:9-17; 12:17) Thus from the start in 1935, these "other sheep" also got to know Jehovah "from the least one of them even to the greatest one of them."

[11] In what way, however, is Christian knowledge of Jehovah different from and better than the knowledge that the Jews had under the old Mosaic Law covenant? The heavenly Maker of the new covenant goes on to tell us: "For I shall forgive their error, and their sin I shall remember no more." (Jeremiah 31:34; Hebrews 8:12) This is due to the fact that the new covenant is based upon a better sacrifice by means of a better Me-

---

10. (a) So under what designation did the remnant of spiritual Israelites begin to welcome the "other sheep"? (b) What knowledge did the "other sheep" acquire?
11. How is Christian knowledge of Jehovah different from and better than that of the Jews under the Law covenant?

diator. (Hebrews 8:6; 9:11, 12, 22, 23) The better sacrifice of the better Mediator needs no repeating, as on the annual Day of Atonement under the old Mosaic Law covenant. (Hebrews 10:15-18) In view of all of this, the knowledge of Jehovah possessed by those in and under the new covenant is indeed better, more enriching, more discerning, more complete than the knowledge of God that the Jews had under the Law covenant.

[12] Above all, Jehovah God, the Covenant-Maker, is the King over those whom he takes into the new covenant and over those whom he places under it. (Matthew 5:34, 35; Jeremiah 10:7) The apostle Paul, 1,850 years before Jesus was enthroned as King in the heavens in 1914, pointed to Jehovah's kingship over those obeying the laws of the new covenant, saying: "Now to the King of eternity, incorruptible, invisible, the only God, be honor and glory forever and ever. Amen."—1 Timothy 1:17.

The Millennial Kingdom After "the Great Tribulation"

[13] The "great crowd" of "other sheep," who are not in the new covenant but are under it, look forward to coming out alive from "the great tribulation." After this present doomed system of things is destroyed, they will enjoy, for a thou-

12. Above all, what position does Jehovah occupy toward those taken into the new covenant and those under it?
13. (a) When and under what circumstances will the "great crowd" in full measure enter into the blessings flowing from the new covenant? (b) What grand purpose will the new covenant have achieved?

The good news of God's Kingdom will be preached throughout the earth before this system ends

sand years, the reign of Jesus Christ and his joint heirs over the cleansed earth. (Revelation 7:9-14) Then the purpose of the new covenant will have been achieved, that of producing "a people for special possession" to become heirs of God's heavenly Kingdom. (1 Peter 2:9; Acts 15:14) By means of God's Kingdom, blessings will flow in full measure to the "great crowd" of surviving "other sheep." Satan the Devil and his invisible demon organization will have been abyssed and will be unable to interfere.—Revelation 21:1-4; 20:1-3.

[14] The surviving "great crowd" of "other sheep" will have had good preparation for taking up life in the new system of things. Like the remnant of spiritual Israelites, they will have come to know

---

14. What good preparation will the surviving "great crowd" have had?

God "from the least one of them even to the greatest one of them." (Jeremiah 31:34) In prayer to God, the reigning King once said: "This means everlasting life, their taking in knowledge of you, the only true God, and of the one whom you sent forth, Jesus Christ." (John 17:3) So this universal knowledge of Jehovah God will work out for everlasting salvation. This will be true not only for the "flesh" that will be saved alive out of the "great tribulation" but also for the billions of human dead ones who will hear the voice of the King and come forth from their memorial tombs. All needed knowledge of Jehovah will be imparted to such resurrected ones.—Matthew 24:21, 22; John 5: 28, 29; Revelation 20:11-15.

[15] Happily, the carrying out of God's new covenant to grand success will not result in loss to the "great crowd" of sheeplike ones who survive the destruction of this doomed system of things. Rather, it will open up the way for even grander blessings here on the cleansed earth that will be theirs to inherit and that they will have an initial part in transforming into a global paradise. (Matthew 25:34; Luke 23:43) Shortly now, those ruining the earth will be gone, "but those hoping in Jehovah are the ones that will possess the earth. . . . The meek ones themselves will possess the earth, and they will indeed find their exquisite delight in the abundance of peace." (Psalm 37: 9-11) All hail the Millennial Kingdom of Jehovah God by the "Prince of Peace" that follows the carrying out of the new covenant!

---

15. Why will the carrying out of the new covenant not result in any loss to the "great crowd" of the "other sheep"?

Chapter 15

Antitypical, Modern-Day Edom to Be Cleared Away

TODAY the world is more mightily armed than ever before. The nuclear weapons of the nations are a real threat to the very existence of mankind. How, then, does the Creator of the human family, Jehovah God, view the situation? This is plainly stated in chapter 34 of Isaiah's prophecy, which opens up with the words:

2 "Come up close, you nations, to hear; and you national groups, pay attention. Let the earth and that which fills it listen, the productive land and all its produce. For Jehovah has indignation against all the nations, and rage against all their army. He must devote them to destruction; he must give them to the slaughter. And their slain ones will be thrown out; and as for their carcasses, their stink will ascend; and the mountains must melt because of their blood. And all those of the army of the heavens must rot away. And the heavens [ineffectual human governments] must be rolled up, just like a book scroll; and their army will all shrivel away, just as the leafage shrivels off the vine and like a shriveled fig off the fig tree." (Isaiah 34:1-4) A dire prophecy indeed!

1, 2. How does the Creator view the mightily armed nations, and what is Jehovah's determination, according to Isaiah's prophecy?

Christendom will receive a judgment similar to that of the Edomites, descendants of Esau, who sold his birthright for a single meal

[3] The Creator of the universe has a controversy with the nations today. That is why the nations are called upon to listen to the Bible-based message that he has caused to be proclaimed worldwide since 1919. They should listen to what he has to say by means of his Witnesses. But the trend of world events proves that they have not done so, and his Witnesses have not been taken seriously by the nations, who opted for the United Nations and not for the heavenly Kingdom in the hands of his enthroned Son, the "Prince of Peace."

---

3. (a) To what are the nations called upon to listen, and why can Jehovah thus rightly command them? (b) What shows that the nations have not listened?

Isaiah's Prophecy Against Edom

[4] Operating among today's national groups is a particularly responsible element. That element was typified by the nation of Edom, which is specifically named in this prophecy. The Edomites were descendants of Esau, who sold his birthright to his twin brother, Jacob, for "bread and lentil stew." It was on that occasion that Esau came to be called Edom, meaning "Red." (Genesis 25: 24-34) Because Jacob supplanted him in the precious birthright, Esau became filled with hate toward his twin brother. Edom became the implacable enemy of the ancient nation of Israel, or Jacob, even though they were twin-brother nations. For this hostility against God's people, Edom incurred the deserved wrath of Jehovah, the God of Israel, and He decreed the eternal annihilation of Edom. This divine determination is set forth in the words of the prophet Isaiah:

[5] "For in the heavens my sword will certainly be drenched. Look! Upon Edom it will descend, and upon the people devoted by me to destruction in justice. Jehovah has a sword; it must be filled with blood; it must be made greasy with the fat, with the blood of young rams and he-goats, with the fat of the kidneys of rams. For Jehovah has a sacrifice in Bozrah [Edom's most prominent city], and a great slaughtering in the land of Edom."—Isaiah 34:5, 6.

4, 5. (a) Who were the Edomites, and what attitude did they take toward their twin-brother nation, Israel? (b) What did Jehovah therefore decree concerning Edom?

[6] The land of the murder-minded nation of Edom must be drenched with their own blood by means of the "sword" of Jehovah. Edom occupied a high, mountainous region. (Jeremiah 49:16) So in causing a slaughter to take place in that land, Jehovah could pictorially say that he was wielding his sword of judgment "in the heavens." Edom was strongly militarized, and its armed forces roved through heaven-high mountain ranges to safeguard the country against invaders. So the army of Edom could fittingly be called "the army of the heavens." But powerful Edom furnished no aid to its twin-brother nation, Israel, when it was attacked by the armies of Babylon. Rather, Edom rejoiced to see the overthrow of the kingdom of Judah and even urged on her devastators. (Psalm 137:7) Edom's treachery went to the point of chasing down individuals running for their lives and handing them over to the enemy. (Obadiah 10-14) The Edomites planned to take over the abandoned country of the Israelites, speaking boastfully against Jehovah.—Ezekiel 35:10-15.

[7] Did Jehovah, the God of ancient Israel, overlook this unbrotherly conduct on the part of the Edomites toward his chosen people? No. That is why God's heart entertained the purpose of "a day of vengeance" and "a year of retributions" in repayment for what had maliciously been done to

---

6. (a) Why could Jehovah speak of wielding his "sword" against Edom "in the heavens"? (b) When the kingdom of Judah was attacked by Babylon, what unbrotherly attitude did Edom display toward Jehovah's people?

7. How did the God of Israel view the treacherous conduct of the nation of Edom?

his earthly organization, called Zion. Said the prophecy: "For Jehovah has a day of vengeance, a year of retributions for the legal case [before the Court of the Universe] over Zion."—Isaiah 34:8; Ezekiel 25:12-14.

8 Not long after the destruction of Jerusalem, Jehovah began expressing his righteous vengeance upon the Edomites by means of the king of Babylon, Nebuchadnezzar. (Jeremiah 25:8, 15, 17, 21) When Babylon's armies moved against Edom, nothing could save the Edomites! Babylon's armies tumbled the Edomites from their rocky heights. It was "a year of retributions" upon Edom. As Jehovah foretold through another prophet: "Because of the violence to your brother Jacob, shame will cover you, and you will have to be cut off to time indefinite. . . . In the way that you have done, it will be done to you. Your sort of treatment will return upon your own head." —Obadiah 10, 15.

9 This also reflects Jehovah's attitude toward the antitypical modern-day Edom. Who is that? Well, in the 20th century, who has taken the lead in reviling and persecuting Jehovah's servants? Has it not been apostate Christendom through its proud clergy class? Yes! Christendom, the realm of false Christianity, has elevated herself to mountain heights in the affairs of this world. She is a lofty part of the organization of mankind's

---

8. (a) Whom did Jehovah use to bring punishment upon Edom? (b) What did the prophet Obadiah foretell regarding Edom?
9. Who is antitypical modern-day Edom, and why?

system of things, and her religions form the dominant part of Babylon the Great. But Jehovah has decreed "a year of retributions" against antitypical, modern-day Edom for outrageous misconduct toward his people, his Witnesses.

A Fate Like That of Edom

10 As we consider the further part of this prophecy of Isaiah, we can have Christendom of today in mind: "Her torrents must be changed into pitch, and her dust into sulphur; and her land must become as burning pitch. By night or by day it will not be extinguished; to time indefinite its smoke will keep ascending." (Isaiah 34:9, 10) The land of Edom is thus portrayed as becoming so parched that it was as if its torrent valleys were running with pitch and as if its dust were sulphur, and then these combustible substances were set afire.—Compare Revelation 17:16.

11 Isaiah's prophecy continues: "From generation to generation she will be parched; forever and ever no one will be passing across her. And the pelican and the porcupine must take possession of her, and long-eared owls and ravens themselves will reside in her; and he must stretch out over her the measuring line of emptiness and the stones of wasteness. Her nobles—there are none there whom they will call to the kingship itself, and her very princes will all become nothing. On

---

10. How does Isaiah 34:9, 10 describe the fate of Edom, but to whom does the prophecy apply today?

11, 12. From the prophetic description given at Isaiah 34:10-15, what would become of the land of Edom, and how long would such state of the land continue?

her dwelling towers thorns must come up, nettles and thorny weeds in her fortified places; and she must become an abiding place of jackals, the courtyard for the ostriches. And haunters of waterless regions must meet up with howling animals, and even the goat-shaped demon will call to its companion. Yes, there the nightjar will certainly take its ease and find for itself a resting-place. There the arrow snake has made its nest and lays eggs."—Isaiah 34:10-15.

12 Edom would become a land of "emptiness" as far as humans were concerned. It was to become a wasteland with only wild beasts, birds, and snakes in it. This parched state of the land was to continue, as verse 10 says, "forever and ever." There was to be no restoration of its former residents.—Obadiah 18.

13 What a terrible plight this foreshadowed for the modern-day counterpart of Edom—Christendom! She has proved herself to be the bitter enemy of Jehovah God, whose Witnesses she has viciously persecuted. So this impending destruction of her prior to Armageddon has been foretold in "the book of Jehovah." (Isaiah 34:16) Specifically, this "book of Jehovah" is his book of accounts, detailing the accounts that he has to settle with those who are his enemies and the oppressors of his people. What was written in "the book of Jehovah" concerning ancient Edom came true, and this guarantees that the prophecy as applying to Christendom, the modern-day Edom, will likewise come true.

---

13. What is foretold for Christendom in "the book of Jehovah," and what, specifically, is this book?

[14] The antitypical Edomites of today have not accepted Jehovah God as King during this "conclusion of the system of things." Moreover, since Christendom is such an outstanding part of Babylon the Great, she is doomed to partake of her plagues. She has not complied with Jehovah's command to "get out of" Babylon the Great. (Revelation 18:4) She has not copied the example of the remnant of spiritual Israelites or that of the "great crowd" of "other sheep."

[15] Christendom's immediate future is bleak indeed. She is doing all she can to pacify her political friends and to keep them from massing together in aggressive action against her, to her utter destruction, but to no avail!

[16] According to Revelation chapters 17 and 18, the Almighty God, Jehovah, will put it into their hearts to give their political and military strength to beastly action against Babylon the Great in all her religious components, including Christendom. This will rid the whole earth of fake Christianity. Christendom's situation will become like that of the bleak condition described in Isaiah 34. She will not be on hand to experience the all-decisive "war of the great day of God the Almighty" against the nations, who will have despoiled Babylon the Great. Antitypical Edom, Christendom, will be totally cleared off the surface of the earth, "forever and ever."

---

14. What have the antitypical Edomites of today not accepted, and what example of Jehovah's people have they failed to follow?

15, 16. What is Christendom's immediate future, as foretold in Revelation 17 and 18 and Isaiah 34?

Chapter 16

The "Great Crowd" Now Takes the "Highway" to God's Organization

DURING the Millennial Reign of the "Prince of Peace," many of the features of Isaiah chapter 35, now undergoing fulfillment before the destruction of Babylon the Great, will have a reflection in a literal sense upon mankind. For what will have been accomplished in a spiritual way will certainly be accomplished in a physical way. The major spiritual fulfillment of this prophecy is taking place right now, with the restoration of God's servants from captivity to Babylon the Great. The prophet Isaiah described it in this lovely phraseology:

2 "The wilderness and the waterless region will exult, and the desert plain will be joyful and blossom as the saffron. Without fail it will blossom, and it will really be joyful with joyousness and with glad crying out. The glory of Lebanon itself must be given to it, the splendor of Carmel and of Sharon. There will be those who will see the glory of Jehovah."—Isaiah 35:1, 2.

3 Where were the wilderness and waterless re-

1, 2. When does Isaiah chapter 35 have a spiritual fulfillment, and what description do the first two verses give?

3. Back in the sixth century B.C.E., where was the barren land, and how could it exult?

gion and desert plain located? In the sixth century B.C.E., they were in the territory of the kingdom of Judah. By 537 B.C.E., that land had lain desolate and without inhabitants for 70 years. But how could a wilderness exult? It would be necessary for the former occupants to be moved back into it. It was to be elevated from its low state and to be given the dignity of the tall mountains of impressive-looking Lebanon.

Producing a Figurative Garden of Eden

4 The modern-day correspondency, in a spiritual sense, to this transformation of a land from a God-forsaken appearance to a condition evidencing Jehovah's restored favor began to take place in 1919. Jehovah's restored people were determined to take full advantage of the peace period that had then opened up. The Greater Cyrus, Jesus Christ, and his Father, Jehovah God, assigned the liberated remnant of spiritual Israelites to do a magnificent work that corresponded to the rebuilding of the temple of Jehovah by the repatriated remnant of ancient Israel after 537 B.C.E. The rehabilitation activities after 1919 resulted in the producing of a figurative garden of Eden.

5 This had been foretold in these words of Isaiah 35: "At that time the eyes of the blind ones will be opened, and the very ears of the deaf ones will be unstopped. At that time the lame one will climb

---

4, 5. (a) When, in modern times, did a similar transformation of such a forsaken land take place, and why? (b) In what did the rehabilitation activities of the anointed remnant result? (c) How did Isaiah 35:5-7 describe their renewed spiritual condition?

up just as a stag does, and the tongue of the speechless one will cry out in gladness. For in the wilderness waters will have burst out, and torrents in the desert plain. And the heat-parched ground will have become as a reedy pool, and the thirsty ground as springs of water. In the abiding place of jackals, a resting-place for them, there will be green grass with reeds and papyrus plants."—Isaiah 35:5-7.

6 The existence of antitypical, modern-day Edom has not prevented the restoration of spiritual Israel to a paradise condition in fulfillment of Isaiah chapter 35. So the modern-day Edomites have no reason to rejoice as the reinstated remnant of spiritual Israel does, along with the increasing "great crowd." The "great crowd" have a large part in maintaining the spiritual paradise of Jehovah's modern-day Witnesses.

7 Never before the end of the Gentile Times had the eyes of understanding of the spiritual Israelites been opened to see that the world trouble that was due to break out in 1914 would terminate with a remnant of them still here on earth. Nor did they see that they and the "great crowd" of "other sheep" would be favored with the privilege of giving a worldwide witness to the establishment of God's Messianic Kingdom. So it occurred that in 1919 the spiritually blind eyes of the remnant

---

6. What has the continued existence of antitypical, modern-day Edom not prevented, and who today cry out exultantly with the restored remnant?

7. What had the remnant's eyes of understanding never envisioned before 1914, but were their "blind" eyes opened?

were opened, and what a vision of the immediate future those opened eyes perceived!

8 At their conventions in Cedar Point, Ohio, in 1919 and 1922, they received some intimation of the work that lay ahead. They bounded to the task before them. Their spiritual ears were unstopped to hear the electrifying message of the Kingdom of God and the need to advertise it. Like a stag, they fairly leaped to serve as witness bearers in behalf of that long-prayed-for Kingdom. Their tongues, which had hitherto been mute, cried out in gladness about the Messianic Kingdom in power in the heavens.—Revelation 14:1-6.

9 Yes, it was as if waters had broken out in a spiritual estate that had formerly lain dry and waste, so that now everything looked green with abundant verdure—ready to be most productive. No wonder that the reinstated people of Jehovah rejoiced exuberantly and felt strengthened like a stag that vigorously climbs up onto the heights! Indeed, the waters of truth about the Kingdom of God, established in the hands of Jesus Christ in 1914, gushed forth with increasing force, resulting in tremendous refreshment.—Isaiah 44:1-4.

The "Highway" of Holiness

10 What does the foregoing signify? This: First

---

8. What effect did the two Cedar Point, Ohio, conventions have on the spiritual ears and tongues of the restored remnant?

9. Spiritually, how was it that waters burst out in the wilderness?

10, 11. (a) What did this refreshing change signify? (b) By what route did the remnant attain to their spiritual paradise, and how does Isaiah 35:8, 9 describe it?

the remnant and later the "great crowd" of "other sheep" have got out of Babylon the Great and have been made God's Kingdom witnesses. But by what route were they to get back into divine favor and get ushered into this spiritual paradise? It was to be as if a broad, spacious roadway were opened to them to permit throngs of pioneer-spirited Israelites to march unitedly together to their God-given homeland. Isaiah's rapturous prophecy indicates this:

[11] "And there will certainly come to be a highway there, even a way; and the Way of Holiness it will be called. The unclean one will not pass over it. And it will be for the one walking on the way, and no foolish ones will wander about on it. No lion will prove to be there, and the rapacious sort of wild beasts will not come up on it."—Isaiah 35:8, 9.

[12] The end of World War I did not automatically open up a modern-day "highway." Eight of the headquarters staff of the Watch Tower Society were still imprisoned and the witness work was seriously slowed. On January 4, 1919, at the annual meeting of the Watch Tower Society in Pittsburgh, Pennsylvania, J. F. Rutherford, the Society's president, was voted back into office, despite his imprisonment, in the certainty that he was an innocent servant of the Most High God.

[13] On March 25, 1919, he and his seven fellow

---

12. Did the end of World War I automatically open up the "highway" for the remnant, and what took place on the fourth day of the year 1919?

13, 14. What events in 1919 indicated that a figurative highway had opened up to the remnant, and who walked upon that "highway"?

prisoners were released and later completely exonerated. *The Watch Tower* of September 15, 1919, page 283, contained the encouraging news that the offices of the Society would, as of October 1, 1919, be moved from Pittsburgh back to Brooklyn Bethel at 124 Columbia Heights. Then, with the December 15, 1919, issue of *The Watch Tower,* this semimonthly publication was announced as again being published in Brooklyn, New York.

14 So it was that in 1919 a figurative highway was opened up to the joyful servants of God. Those who wanted to be holy in Jehovah's sight were the ones who walked upon that "highway," "the Way of Holiness." Any who did not have the right objective, a clean motive, did not strike out on that figurative "Way of Holiness" and attain to reinstatement in divine favor.

15 On June 1, 1935, at the convention in Washington, D.C., 840 of the "great crowd" were baptized in water, giving visual proof that they had begun to enter the "highway." Now, increasing millions of them have entered that highway, joining the diminishing numbers of the anointed remnant. Peacefully and in enjoyable companionship, they now walk together on the "highway," determined that, with the help of Almighty God in heaven, nothing shall break up their unity.

16 Figuratively speaking, no lion or any other rapacious beast was to be found on this highway.

---

15. What furnishes visual proof that the "great crowd" has entered the figurative highway?
16. Figuratively speaking, how is it that there is no lion or other rapacious beast on this highway?

That is, there was nothing to act as a deterrent or to frighten off the anointed remnant and the "great crowd." They launched out confidently on the route that their Liberator, the Greater Cyrus, now opened up to them, with Zion as their destination.

[17] Today, so deep into "the conclusion of the system of things," that divinely provided "highway" remains open. Throngs of appreciative people are acting upon the information that Babylon the Great has fallen before the onslaught of the Greater Cyrus, Jesus Christ. And they are fleeing from it, entering in upon the spiritual paradise route, "the Way of Holiness."—Jeremiah 50:8.

[18] They are attaining to indescribable joy and gladness, as the closing verse of Isaiah chapter 35 puts it: "And the very ones redeemed by Jehovah will return and certainly come to Zion with a joyful cry; and rejoicing to time indefinite will be upon their head. To exultation and rejoicing they will attain, and grief and sighing must flee away." Their grief and sighing over having once been out of harmony with Jehovah God have fled away since 1919. And grief and sighing have not returned to Jehovah's faithful, joyful witnesses. Thanks be to the truthtelling God, Jehovah, who has so praiseworthily fulfilled that glowing prophecy of Isaiah chapter 35!

---

17. (a) Though we are deep into "the conclusion of the system of things," is the "highway" still open? (b) Who are entering upon "the Way of Holiness," and how have they done so?
18. How does the last verse of Isaiah 35 describe the present situation of Jehovah's faithful witnesses, and to whom go the thanks for the fulfillment of this prophecy?

Chapter 17

Loyally Remembering Jehovah's Organization

MUCH is said today about loyalty to one's country. But how much do the rulers and peoples of this world say about loyalty to God, who is the Creator of the land occupied by one's country? In ancient times, King David of Israel was a loyal worshiper of the Creator, Jehovah God. Addressing this loyal God, David said these words to him: "With someone loyal you will act in loyalty." (2 Samuel 22:26; Psalm 18:25) Do those words express your attitude toward God?

[2] The general attitude of mankind today is not one of great concern about loyalty to God. But regardless of this, Jehovah is loyal to the human family. He has not cast it away. His loyal Son said: "God loved the world so much that he gave his only-begotten Son, in order that everyone exercising faith in him might not be destroyed but have everlasting life." (John 3:16) God did not abandon the world of mankind to its greatest adversary, Satan, who had induced our first parents to turn disloyal to God. God also showed his loyalty to the human family in 2370 B.C.E. by preserving Noah

1. We should be thinking about loyalty to whom, and what did King David say in this regard?
2. How do we know that Jehovah has remained loyal to the human family?

and his family through the worldwide deluge that wiped out all the rest of mankind. (2 Peter 2:5) In this way the Creator gave a new start to the human family.

[3] Today the violence earth wide outrivals that of Noah's time over 4,000 years ago. (Genesis 6:11) So there is justification for the same God to wipe out of existence the present worldly system of things. This he has purposed to do, but when doing so, he will not destroy his loyal ones on earth. He will then live up to Psalm 37:28: "Jehovah is a lover of justice, and he will not leave his loyal ones." As in Noah's day, he will give a righteous introduction to the new system of things composed of "new heavens and a new earth." (2 Peter 3:13) The reward for loyalty is great. It is life giving!

[4] During the reign of King David, the nation of Israel proved to be loyal to Jehovah. David set the pattern for the whole nation. That nation was Jehovah's visible organization. They were an organized people that were peculiarly his own. No doubt that is what is meant by God's reminder, as set out in Amos 3:1, 2: "Hear this word that Jehovah has spoken concerning you, O sons of Israel, concerning the whole family that I brought up out of the land of Egypt, saying, 'You people only have I known out of all the families of the ground.'"—Compare 1 Kings 8:41-43.

---

3. (a) What can be said about violence today, and what has God purposed to do about it? (b) What is the reward for loyalty to Jehovah?

4. How do we know that the nation of Israel was Jehovah's visible organization of that time?

5 In parallel with this fact of Bible history, this same God, Jehovah, has an organized people, a visible organization, on earth today. It is an organization that is exclusively his own. However, attempts were made to introduce errors into God's organization even at its beginning during the days of the apostles of Jesus Christ, who were stout defenders of the integrity of the Christian congregation. (1 Corinthians 15:12; 2 Timothy 2:16-18) Following the death of the apostle John, evidently not long after 98 C.E., the predicted falling away set in.—Acts 20:30; 2 Peter 2:1, 3; 1 Timothy 4:1.

6 This apostasy dominated for more than 17 centuries, into the latter half of the 19th century. By then Christendom had become fragmented into hundreds of religious sects. The identification of the true people of God was blurred. Christendom was a babel of religious organizations, large and small, speaking a hodgepodge of religious languages not solidly based on the religious language of the inspired Scriptures. Such religious organizations had really been taken captive by an empire that was far greater than the Babylonian Empire that destroyed Jerusalem. But what was ancient Babylon like, and what must have been the attitude of faithful Jews held captive?

---

5. (a) During the days of the apostles of Jesus Christ, were efforts made to introduce errors into the Christian congregation? (b) What was foretold to happen after the death of the apostles?
6. (a) How long did the apostasy dominate, and with what result? (b) Into what captivity did Christendom's religious organizations come, and what questions arise?

Captives in Babylon Loyally Remembered Zion

[7] Ancient Babylon was the land of false gods, the idols of which abounded. (Daniel 5:4) We can imagine the effect that this worship of many false gods had upon the hearts of the faithful Jews who had worshiped only the one true God without any kind of image. Instead of beholding the temple of Jehovah in all its beauty in Jerusalem, they beheld the temples of these false gods and their idols throughout the land of Babylon.* How the worshipers of the one and only true God must have suffered a feeling of revulsion by all of this!

[8] According to the prophecy of Jeremiah, they would have to put up with this for 70 years before restoration would come. (2 Chronicles 36:18-21; Jeremiah 25:11, 12) The heartbroken condition of the Jewish captives who loved Jehovah and desired to worship him at a temple dedicated to him at his chosen city is described for us in Psalm 137:1-4: "By the rivers of Babylon—there we sat down. We also wept when we remembered Zion. Upon the poplar trees in the midst of her we hung

* A cuneiform inscription from ancient Babylon reports: "Altogether there are in Babylon 53 temples of the chief gods, 55 chapels of Marduk, 300 chapels for the earthly deities, 600 for the heavenly deities, 180 altars for the goddess Ishtar, 180 for the gods Nergal and Adad and 12 other altars for different gods."

7. (a) Religiously speaking, what was the land of ancient Babylon like? (b) What effect must this have had on the Jewish captives?
8. (a) How long would the Jews have to put up with their captivity, and what longing would loyal Jews have? (b) How does Psalm 137:1-4 describe the heartbroken condition of the loyal Jewish captives?

Very confuse

revulsion = distasteful

our harps. For there those holding us captive asked us for the words of a song, and those mocking us—for rejoicing: 'Sing for us one of the songs of Zion.' How can we sing the song of Jehovah upon foreign ground?"

[9] "The song of Jehovah" should be the song of a free people worshiping him at his holy temple. To those Babylonians, the singing of "the song of Jehovah" by these Jews in the land of their captivity would be an occasion for the captors to jeer at the name of Jehovah as the name of a god inferior to the gods of Babylon. His holy name had already come under tremendous reproach by his letting his people be taken off their God-given homeland and marched away to a land with a multiplicity of gods. But the time for those Babylonians to jeer at him and to belittle his name people was to be for only a limited period—70 years. Then down with the false gods of Babylon and up with the true God, Jehovah!

Heart Attachment to Jehovah's Organization

[10] Today there is a religious organization called Babylon the Great that is not confined to the land of the original Babylon but that is worldwide. Does the heart attitude of the Jews in ancient Babylon set a correct pattern for Jehovah's people

9. How would the Babylonians regard the singing of "the song of Jehovah," but what was due to happen at the end of the 70 years?
10. What question arises with regard to Jehovah's people of this 20th century who were brought into captivity to Babylon the Great?

of this 20th century who were forcibly brought into captivity to Babylon the Great as a discipline from the God of ancient Israel?

[11] Although they could have settled down in ancient Babylon and made themselves at home, since the exile would be about a generation long, did they let their homeland fade out of memory? The captive psalmist expresses it beautifully when he voices the feelings of his fellow captives: "If I should forget you, O Jerusalem, let my right hand be forgetful. Let my tongue stick to my palate, if I were not to remember you, if I were not to make Jerusalem ascend above my chief cause for rejoicing."—Psalm 137:5, 6. Let him die

[12] What did that heart attitude of the captive Israelite express? This: loyalty to Jehovah's visible organization of that time while he saw the land that God had given to His chosen people lying desolate for 70 years. Yes, the visible organization of Jehovah lived on in the hearts of those Israelites.

[13] Such loyalty to the ancient visible organization of God was duly rewarded. This was when Babylon, the third world power of Bible history, was overturned, and Medo-Persia, the fourth world power, carried out the will of the God of Israel. How? By restoring the captive Jews to the

---

11. (a) Did the loyal Jews let their homeland fade out of memory? (b) How did the captive psalmist express the feelings of his fellow captives?
12. What did the heart attitude of the captive psalmist express?
13. How was loyalty to Jehovah's visible organization rewarded?

land of the visible organization of Jehovah, with instructions to rebuild the temple of their God as the hub of the capital city, Jerusalem. (2 Chronicles 36:22, 23) Not only was the temple of true worship rebuilt but the walled city of Jerusalem was also reconstructed, to become the city from which Jehovah reigned as King over his people.

[14] More than six centuries after Jerusalem's destruction, Jesus said: "Do not swear at all, neither by heaven, because it is God's throne; nor by earth, because it is the footstool of his feet; nor by Jerusalem, because it is the city of the great King." (Matthew 5:34, 35) When the Messiah was on earth, a rebuilt temple of Jehovah stood in Jerusalem, and, symbolically speaking, Jehovah God reigned in the Most Holy of that temple. So from Jerusalem as the capital city of his people, Jehovah reigned over his visible organization.

Jehovah Remains Loyal to His Organization

[15] Well, now, did Jesus cast out God's visible organization when he exposed the unfaithful religious leaders of Israel and denounced them? Yes, for he said: "Jerusalem, Jerusalem, the killer of the prophets and stoner of those sent forth to her, —how often I wanted to gather your children together, the way a hen gathers her chicks to-

14. (a) Centuries later, what did the Messiah say about Jehovah's visible organization? (b) In what sense did Jehovah reign from Jerusalem?

15. Was Jesus rejecting the visible part of Jehovah's organization when he exposed the unfaithful religious leaders of Israel? Explain.

gether under her wings! But you people did not want it. Look! Your house is abandoned to you." (Matthew 23:37, 38) When Jesus rejected Jerusalem and her "children," was he thereby leaving his heavenly Father without an earthly organization? No! For Jesus himself was the foundation of the new visible organization that the Creator of the universe was going to build up.

Just a chance

[16] The rejection of natural Israel was certainly indicated when, at the death of Jesus on the torture stake, the thick curtain that separated the Most Holy from the Holy in the temple of Jerusalem was ripped in two "from top to bottom." At the same time, "the earth quaked, and the rock-masses were split." These were miraculous acts on the part of the God who used to reign there in a typical way, indicating his rejection of the nation of Israel and her religion.—Matthew 27:51.

[17] Prospective members of the new visible organization that Jehovah God was shortly to build up were left there in the domain of Jerusalem. Jesus commended them to the care of God, who was abandoning the earthly city in favor of something superior. (John 17:9-15) Thus Jehovah remained loyal to his organization, showing special consideration for their faithful forefathers, Abraham, Isaac, and Jacob and the 12 sons of Jacob. (Daniel 12:1) The next chapter will pursue further our discussion of loyalty, based on Psalm 137.

---

16. At the time of Jesus' death on the torture stake, how was the rejection of natural Israel indicated?
17. How did Jesus and Jehovah show loyalty to prospective members of the new visible organization of God?

Chapter 18

Loyalty to God's Visible Organization Today

IN PSALM 16:10 it is written: "You will not leave my soul in Sheol. You will not allow your loyal one to see the pit." And in Psalm 50:5 it is written: "Gather to me my loyal ones, those concluding my covenant over sacrifice." Are those who conclude Jehovah's covenant the ones who provide the "sacrifice"? No, these loyal ones do not make an individual "sacrifice" of themselves, giving up their fleshly bodies in order to make a compact with God.

2 How, then, is the covenant concluded? Over the "sacrifice" of the "loyal one" whose soul was not left in Sheol but who was resurrected from the dead. The apostle Peter applied the words of Psalm 16:10 to Jesus Christ and went on to say: "He [David] saw beforehand and spoke concerning the resurrection of the Christ, that neither was he forsaken in Hades nor did his flesh see corruption. This Jesus God resurrected."—Acts 2: 25, 27, 31, 32.

3 This resurrected Jesus is the Mediator of the new covenant, and it is on the basis of his sacrifice

---

1, 2. How is the scripture at Psalm 50:5 to be understood?
3. Who are those gathered according to the command in Psalm 50:5, and why should they be motivated to prove loyal to God?

that the new covenant is validated. (Hebrews 9:15, 17) So who are those to be gathered according to the command in Psalm 50:5? They are Jesus' disciples who are in the new covenant by reason of his sacrifice. Out of gratitude to Jehovah for this incomparable sacrifice, they should be motivated to prove loyal to him.

4 When Jehovah's Kingdom was set up in the heavens in 1914, the nations raged in opposition to that Kingdom by engaging in the first world war, and God permitted this. (Psalm 2:1, 2) Satan the Devil endeavored to use that world conflict to destroy the visible part of Jehovah's organization. He succeeded in having the president of the Watch Tower Bible and Tract Society imprisoned in the federal penitentiary in Atlanta, Georgia. Seven other representatives of the Society were imprisoned with him.

5 Because of persecution, the Society's headquarters in Brooklyn, New York, were moved to a rented building in Pittsburgh, Pennsylvania. This was done to keep up the publication of the *Watch Tower* magazine. The heavenly glorification of the faithful ones was expected shortly. But those of the remnant were inclined to weep as they contemplated the oppressed, crippled condition of Jehovah's organization.—Psalm 137:1.

4, 5. (a) What success did Satan the Devil have during the first world war in his efforts to destroy Jehovah's visible organization? (b) To where was the Society's headquarters moved, and why? (c) In a modern-day parallel to Psalm 137:1, what was the emotional state, or disposition, of the loyal remnant when they contemplated the crippled condition of God's organization?

Loyalty During Time of Imprisonment

6 Displaying loyalty to Jehovah's organization during his time of imprisonment, the president of the Watch Tower Society, J. F. Rutherford, on December 25, 1918, wrote a special letter to J. A. Bohnet, a trusted fellow servant of Jehovah. It was addressed to him at the Society's office in Pittsburgh. Rutherford wrote the following:

7 "Because I refused to compromise with Babylon, but faithfully tried to serve my Lord, I am in prison, for which I am thankful. . . . I would far prefer His approval and smile and be in prison, than to compromise with or yield to the Beast and be free and have the plaudits of the whole world. It is a blessed, sweet experience to suffer for faithful service to the Lord. In the Kingdom we shall prize the Father's smile above all things. This should be uppermost in the mind of every child of God. We are longing for the union that will make us One there. I am happy, yet I long to see you all again. The convention and annual meeting draws near. May the spirit of Christ fill the heart of every attendant . . .

8 "There is yet much to do. It will be a great favor to participate. Only those who love Him supremely are faithful and will be thus honored. . . . Before that glad day there must be a strenuous witness given. . . . Past methods and means will not meet the requirements, but the Lord in His own good way will provide. . . . I am glad this

6-8. During his imprisonment, how did the Society's president, J. F. Rutherford, display loyalty to Jehovah's organization?

prison experience was reserved for us rather than for Brother Russell. Never before have I so thoroughly hated iniquity and loved righteousness and longed to help others. . . . Zion's triumph is at hand."

God's Organization Their "Chief Cause for Rejoicing"

[9] Although Jehovah's servants were branded in the world as disloyal, traitors, and unpatriotic, they did not renounce Jehovah's organization. They refused to compromise under that pressure. They would rather lose the use of their right hand or become mute than forget God's organization and no longer let it be their "chief cause for rejoicing."—Psalm 137:5, 6.

[10] Jehovah's enemies maliciously rejoiced over the action against the earthly representatives of his universal organization. But Jehovah's servants prayed for his day of vengeance to come because of all this affront heaped upon his organization. They took up the words that the psalmist spoke with reference to ancient Edom: "Remember, O Jehovah, regarding the sons of Edom the day of Jerusalem, who were saying: 'Lay it bare! Lay it bare to the foundation within it!'" (Psalm 137:7; Galatians 4:26) Ah, no, Jehovah loves his wifelike organization too dearly to forget what those who are part of the Devil's organization say

9. What attitude of the psalmist did the imprisoned representatives of the Society reflect?
10, 11. (a) For what did the loyal remnant pray, and what words of the psalmist did they take up regarding Edom? (b) What had the enemies of Jehovah's visible organization been able to do, and what did such enemies never expect?

and do against the loyal ones of his earthly organization.

[11] To all outward appearances at that time, such political sympathizers with Babylon the Great did lay Jehovah's visible organization "bare to the foundation within it." They never expected to see it rise from the dust to the worldwide organization that it is today.

The Happiness of His Avenger

[12] Jehovah used the Persian ruler Cyrus to liberate his people from the ancient world power Babylon. But in the fullest sense, Cyrus was not the one meant in the closing words of Psalm 137, which refer to Babylon the Great, the world empire of false religion: "O daughter of Babylon, who are to be despoiled, happy will he be that rewards you with your own treatment with which you treated us. Happy will he be that grabs ahold and does dash to pieces your children against the crag."—Psalm 137:8, 9.

[13] Who will be that "happy" one? Does the "happy" one stand for the symbolic "ten horns" that are upon the head of the "wild beast," on the back of which the old harlot system of religion has ridden with such pomp for so long? No, because the political destroyers of the world empire of false religion do not destroy it to make way for

---

12. (a) Who proved to be the liberator of Jehovah's captive people in ancient Babylon, and does Psalm 137:8, 9 refer to him in the fullest sense? (b) What did these verses foretell about the avenger of God's earthly organization?
13, 14. Why could the "happy" one of Psalm 137:8, 9 not refer to the political powers that destroy Babylon the Great?

the pure worship of the true God. They do not do it for the glory of the God of the Bible. How, then, could such ones actually be the "happy" one designated by the psalmist?

14 The political powers of this world do not accomplish this antireligious work out of love for Jehovah's worshipers. Why not? Because Jehovah's Witnesses will stand in the way of their producing an exclusively godless world. So the political powers are merely the instruments used by the God of the Witnesses to carry out his own purpose.—Revelation 17:17.

15 Thus, though these political powers may be directly used in the annihilation of the world empire of false religion, it is really Jehovah God who is motivating them. How? He uses his empowered royal Son, the Greater Cyrus, Jesus Christ. Thus, Jesus Christ in Kingdom power is the "happy" one foretold by the psalmist!

16 Whereas Jehovah will safeguard his loyal ones, he will, in a figurative sense, grab ahold of every one of the religious "children" of the harlot-like system of false teaching and break them to pieces against what looms up like a "crag"—the unyielding Kingdom of Jehovah God by Jesus Christ.

17 When he was on earth, Jesus was anointed with the spirit of his divine Backer not only "to

15. Who really motivates the political powers, and by means of whom?
16. How does Jehovah destroy Babylon's "children"?
17. (a) According to Isaiah 61:1, 2, what was Jesus to proclaim after being anointed with God's spirit? (b) How is the proclamation being carried out today?

proclaim the year of goodwill on the part of Jehovah" but also to proclaim "the day of vengeance on the part of our God." (Isaiah 61:1, 2; Luke 4: 16-21) In our time, during "the last days" of this system of things, Jehovah is having his faithful servants proclaim "the day of vengeance on the part of our God" in all the inhabited earth for a warning to all the nations. In this proclamation the remnant have been joined by a growing "great crowd" of sheeplike disciples of Jesus Christ, as forevisioned in Revelation 7:9-17.

[18] All of these, the remnant and the "great crowd," have obeyed the angelic command of Revelation 18:4. They have got out of Babylon the Great. Why is such action urgent? Because they must flee out of Babylon the Great before her religious "children" are broken to pieces and devastated by means of the "wild beast" and its "ten horns" right before Armageddon. These loyal ones will share in the happiness of the Greater Cyrus, Jesus Christ. They will join the heavens in saying: "Praise Jah, you people! The salvation and the glory and the power belong to our God, because his judgments are true and righteous. For he has executed judgment upon the great harlot who corrupted the earth with her fornication." —Revelation 19:1, 2; compare Jeremiah 51:8-11.

[19] Since 1919 Jehovah has done "a great thing" for his people. (Psalm 126:1-3) For this magnifying of his power of liberation, demonstrating that he is "the *faithful* God," the liberated remnant are

---

18. In what happiness will God's loyal ones share?
19. What happiness does the loyal remnant now enjoy, and what greater happiness awaits them?

still glad at heart. (Deuteronomy 7:9) They are profoundly happy, but there is the greater happiness that awaits them. This will be when they can join in the happiness of the Greater Cyrus, the reigning Monarch, Jesus Christ, at the time when he breaks to pieces all the "children" of that devilish organization.

[20] Millions of former "captives" of Babylon the Great have already been helped to flee that doomed religious organization before its violent destruction. The result has been the "great crowd" of "other sheep." They now number, earth wide, more than 3,000,000, with no limit to the number yet to be rescued from the destruction of the worldwide empire of false religion. In loyalty to Jehovah's organization, they are sharing the happiness of the remnant by joining them in proclaiming Jehovah's day of vengeance upon religious Babylon the Great.

[21] Let there, then, be no compromise with that world empire of false religion. Let there be no returning to her in these days of her decline. May we keep on helping as many captives of Babylon the Great as possible to get out of that doomed system before the Greater Cyrus gains his happifying victory.

---

20. Who else are sharing in the happiness of the anointed remnant, and why?
21. What should be our attitude toward Babylon the Great and her captives?

Chapter 19

The Impending "War of the Great Day of God the Almighty"

THE NATIONS have at long last come to the time when they are obliging Almighty God to write the grand finale to "the book of the Wars of Jehovah." (Numbers 21:14) That literal book was a record of the wars that Jehovah fought on behalf of his people. Evidently Moses read it. The book may have had its beginning with Abraham's successful warfare against the kings who captured Lot, with Jehovah fighting for Abraham. (Genesis 14:1-16, 20) Soon now, "the book of the Wars of Jehovah" will be brought to a grand climax with a new chapter added—the account of his most glorious victory. That will be "the war of the great day of God the Almighty" at Armageddon, the finale with regard to this system of things. (Revelation 16:14, 16) The entire "book" will show that Almighty God has never lost a fight, or battle.

2 True, from the beginning of Christianity until now, Jehovah has safeguarded his people by means other than military wars. Never has Jeho-

---

1. (a) What will the nations soon oblige Almighty God to write in "the book of the Wars of Jehovah," and what was that book? (b) With what war will that book reach a grand climax?
2, 3. (a) Since the beginning of Christianity, what has been true as to Jehovah's fighting military "wars"? (b) What will provoke Jehovah into fighting for his servants in our time?

vah fought for his Christian witnesses as he did for Israel under the Mosaic Law. But the time will come in the near future when he will militarily fight for his devoted servants of modern times. What will provoke that war at Armageddon?

3 Prior to the outbreak of God's war, Babylon the Great, the world empire of false religion, will have been destroyed. Satan the Devil and the irreligious political demolishers of Babylon the Great will resent the fact that Jehovah's Witnesses will be the only religious group to survive. World rulers will not have attained their goal of a godless world. So, now, forward to the all-out attack upon the worshipers of Jehovah, whose universal sovereignty they deny and defy! Thus they will actually be fighting against God.—Revelation 17:14, 16; compare Acts 5:39.

"Jehovah of Armies" Resumes Military Activities

4 Satan the Devil, the symbolic Gog of Magog, will mastermind this attack on Jehovah's people. When Gog uses his atheistic hordes to attack Jehovah's people, to plunder and destroy them, Jehovah will step in and fight for his people, as foretold at Ezekiel 38:2, 12, 18-20. Jehovah's response is also foretold at Zechariah 14:3: "Jehovah will certainly go forth and war against those nations as in the day of his warring, in the day of fight." In this way the God of the Bible will give a

---

4. (a) How does Jehovah respond to Gog's attack? (b) What will that response prove, in harmony with the name "Jehovah of armies"?

witness to all the modern nations that he still is a Warrior God, just as he was in the days of ancient Israel, when, as recorded in the Hebrew Scriptures, he was described as "Jehovah of armies" 260 times.—Psalm 24:10; 84:12.

[5] When "the great day of God the Almighty" arrives, it will be the time for "the war" that will mark that day. Jehovah signals his Field Marshal, Jesus Christ. In the name of Jehovah, he and the heavenly armies of myriads of angels plunge into the battle, as if riding upon war horses. (Jude 14, 15) Like a war correspondent, the apostle John gives us an advance account of the smashing victory that Jehovah's Field Marshal will gain in "the war of the great day of God the Almighty":

[6] "I saw the heaven opened, and, look! a white horse. And the one seated upon it is called Faithful and True, and he judges and carries on war in righteousness. His eyes are a fiery flame, and upon his head are many diadems . . . Also, the armies that were in heaven were following him on white horses, and they were clothed in white, clean, fine linen. And out of his mouth there protrudes a sharp long sword, that he may strike the nations with it, and he will shepherd them with a rod of iron. He treads too the winepress of the anger of the wrath of God the Almighty. And upon his outer garment, even upon his thigh, he has a name written, King of kings and Lord of lords."—Revelation 19:11-16.

5, 6. (a) What war now breaks out, and who leads the heavenly armies into battle? (b) What account does the apostle John give of the heavenly armies going into battle?

[7] The royal Field Marshal, Jesus Christ, leads the heavenly armies in a victorious charge against all the combined enemies at Armageddon. He turns that battlefield into a huge winepress! Since the King of kings "treads too the winepress of the anger of the wrath of God the Almighty," this signifies that the nations will be thoroughly squashed. They will be dumped like ripe grapes into the tremendous "winepress," where "the anger of the wrath of God the Almighty" will be brought to bear upon them with crushing effect. The heavenly armies will join in the treading of "the great winepress of the anger of God."—Revelation 14:18-20.

[8] Jehovah's Witnesses on earth do not take up the "sword" against Gog's hordes, but Jehovah does. This is his fight! And now at last the nations of this scientifically advanced world will see him fight! Listen as he describes his war tactics: "'I will call forth against him [Gog] throughout all my mountainous region a sword,' is the utterance of the Sovereign Lord Jehovah. 'Against his own brother the sword of each one will come to be. And I will bring myself into judgment with him, with pestilence and with blood; and a flooding downpour and hailstones, fire and sulphur I shall rain down upon him and upon his bands and upon the many peoples that will be with him. And I shall certainly magnify myself and sanctify myself and make myself known before the eyes of

7. What does the treading of the symbolic winepress of the anger of God signify for the nations?
8. How does Jehovah describe his war tactics?

many nations; and they will have to know that I am Jehovah.'"—Ezekiel 38:21-23.

Divine Weapons Used Against the Enemy

[9] As weapons of warfare, Jehovah will wield the forces of creation: flooding cloudbursts of rain, hailstones of death-dealing size, downpours of streaking fire and sulphur, spouting waters from deep within the earth, and crackling lightnings. At the flashing of God's means of death to his enemies, the light will be so intense by day and by night that the natural sun and moon will appear

---

9. What are some of the weapons of warfare that Jehovah will use against his enemies?

"Jehovah of armies" will war against the nations

to be no longer needed for illumination. It will be as if they stood still, not functioning as light bearers but letting Jehovah's radiant missiles put on a display of illuminating power. (Habakkuk 3: 10, 11) Jehovah has an abundance of natural phenomena at his disposal for fighting.—Joshua 10: 11; Job 38:22, 23, 29.

10 In the coming "day of fight," Jehovah will also use pestilence and "the scourge." The prophet Zechariah wrote about this: "This is what will prove to be the scourge with which Jehovah will scourge all the peoples that will actually do mili-

---

10. According to Zechariah 14:12, what else will Jehovah use in the coming "day of fight"?

tary service against Jerusalem: There will be a rotting away of one's flesh, while one is standing upon one's feet; and one's very eyes will rot away in their sockets, and one's very tongue will rot away in one's mouth."—Zechariah 14:12.

11 Whether "the scourge" will be literal or not, it will silence the mouths that are opened to let out terrifying threats! Tongues rotted away! Powers of vision will cease, so that the fierce-eyed attackers can only strike out blindly. Eyes rotted away! Muscles of mighty warriors will lose strength while they stand on their feet—not while they are lying on the ground as corpses. Flesh that clothes their skeletal structures rotted away!—Compare Habakkuk 3:5.

12 "The scourge" hits suddenly at their military camps. Mobile equipment for the attack is helplessly immobilized! (Zechariah 14:15; compare Exodus 14:24, 25.) Indicating how useless their military equipment will be are the words of Zechariah 14:6: "It must occur in that day that there will prove to be no precious light—things will be congealed." No heavenly light of divine favor will shine upon them. Artificial lights of modern science will not remove the darkness of divine disfavor. Operational things will be immobilized, as if stiffened by cold—congealed.

13 All of this is terrifying enough! But adding to

---

11. What will happen when "the scourge" hits the warriors who are attacking Jehovah's people?
12. How will "the scourge" affect the enemy's military camps and equipment?
13. What will add to the terror that Jehovah stirs up among the attackers?

the terror is the confusion that God will stir up among the attackers. Their unitedness of action against Jehovah's Witnesses will be broken up. Like gladiators with a blinding helmet over their heads in a Roman arena, they will strike at one another sightlessly. The death-dealing confusion will become widespread as they engage in mutual slaughter.—Zechariah 14:13.

14 The mass slaughter on that day of days will be enormous, for the forces lined up on Gog's side in that battle will be tremendous. (Revelation 19: 19-21) That will indeed be a global conflict, for no section of the earth will escape the destruction. Moreover, those slaughtered at Armageddon will not be laid in graves with markers to memorialize them. Birds of every sort and beasts of the field will share in the benefits of God's triumph and, at the same time, help cleanse the earth of the many carcasses that will lie strewed upon the ground like fertilizer, unlamented, unburied, abhorred by the survivors. (Ezekiel 39:1-5, 17-20; Revelation 19:17, 18) "Those slain by Jehovah" will have earned eternal infamy for themselves.—Jeremiah 25:32, 33; Isaiah 66:23, 24.

Jehovah's Name Beautified

15 Thus, "Jehovah of armies" by means of his Field Marshal, Jesus Christ, will gain undying

---

14. (a) How extensive will the slaughter be at that time, and how will the birds and the beasts share in the benefits of Jehovah's victory? (b) What attitude will the survivors have toward "those slain by Jehovah"?
15. What outstanding event will then have been accomplished, and with what effect on Jehovah's name?

glory for himself. The greatest event of universal history will then have been accomplished—the vindication of Jehovah's universal sovereignty and the sanctification of his sacred name. (Ezekiel 38:23; 39:6, 7) Jehovah will make a name for himself surpassing anything that was described in "the book of the Wars of Jehovah" and in the Hebrew Scriptures of the Holy Bible. (Compare Isaiah 63:12-14.) How beautiful a name Jehovah will make for himself by his awe-inspiring victory in "the war of the great day of God the Almighty"! Jubilantly all lovers of that name will then laud it forever, singing forth its praises!

[16] Forward, then, into battle action, O Jehovah of armies, with your royal Son Jesus Christ at your side! (Psalm 110:5, 6) Let your faithful witnesses on earth become the joyous witnesses of your peerless victory by means of your King Jesus Christ at "the war of the great day of God the Almighty." Let the "great crowd" exultantly "come out of the great tribulation" to be your earthly witnesses forever. (Revelation 7:14) Under your loving care, let them survive into the warless Millennial Reign of your victorious "Prince of Peace." Let them be a visible testimony to the resurrected dead in vindication of the sovereignty that is rightly yours over all the universe. Thank you for writing the grand finale to "the book of the Wars of Jehovah." To an eternity of time, let this account of your matchless victory remain in the annals of universal history!

---

16. In view of the impending "war of the great day of God the Almighty," what prayer is offered in behalf of the "great crowd"?

Chapter 20

A Happy Human Family Under a New Fatherhood

AFTER Armageddon, a second fatherhood awaits all mankind. That is indeed good news! The new fatherhood makes possible eternal life in human perfection in an earth-wide paradise, for the new Father of the human family is himself deathless. He has the power to confer perfect life upon all those whom he adopts as his children on earth.

2 A new fatherhood is needed because mankind lost its original fatherhood, the fatherhood of man's Creator. The lineage that runs from Jesus back to the first man, Adam, ends up by giving us this list: "Cainan, son of Enosh, son of Seth, son of Adam, son of God."—Luke 3:37, 38.

3 Loss of the fatherhood of Jehovah God proved tragic for all humankind. The descendants of Adam inherited the condemnation of death. The matter is plainly stated in Romans 5:12: "Through one man sin entered into the world and death through sin, and thus death spread to all men because they had all sinned." That "one man" was Adam, and for his willful sin, he lost the fatherhood of his Creator, Jehovah.

---

1. Why is the subject of a new fatherhood such good news to the human family?
2. Why is a new fatherhood needed?
3. How tragic was the loss of the fatherhood of Jehovah God to all humanity?

[4] Under whose fatherhood did Adam then come? Into whose fatherhood did he bring the world of mankind? It would be the fatherhood of the one who prevailed upon him to step out of the family of all obedient sons of God in heaven and on earth. It was the fatherhood of the one who told the first lie, Satan the Devil. How did that opposer of Jehovah bring this about?

[5] At 2 Corinthians 11:3 the apostle Paul exposes the matter, writing: "The serpent seduced Eve by its cunning." Cunningly, Satan used a serpent in Eden to convey the first lie to unsuspecting Eve, falsely charging Jehovah God with lying. (Genesis 3:1-7; John 8:44) Adam did not correct his wife. He did not refuse to eat with her and did not save the situation. His deliberate misdeed played into the Serpent's hands. Placing the blame where it belonged, 1 Timothy 2:14 states: "Adam was not deceived, but the woman was thoroughly deceived and came to be in transgression."

The One Worthy of Fatherhood

[6] In refusing to worship "the god of this system," Jesus proved that he was the One to be entrusted with the second fatherhood of the human family. (2 Corinthians 4:4; Matthew 4:1-11; Luke 4:1-13) From his human birth in 2 B.C.E., he was the One to whom the prophecy of Isaiah 9:6 applied:

---

4. Under whose fatherhood did Adam and mankind come?
5. (a) What agency did Satan the Devil use to deceive Adam's wife into disobedience to God? (b) Why and how did Adam come under full responsibility for his course of action?
6, 7. With what fatherhood did Jesus show that he could be entrusted, and how did Bible prophecy specify this?

[7] "There has been a child born to us, there has been a son given to us; and the princely rule will come to be upon his shoulder. And his name will be called Wonderful Counselor, Mighty God, Eternal Father, Prince of Peace." So the "Prince of Peace" has another vital role to play for mankind —that of being its "Eternal Father."

[8] The Son of God is to become the "Eternal Father" to this human family, for which he laid down his perfect human life in sacrifice. It is just as the apostle Paul writes: "For if by one man's trespass many died, the undeserved kindness of God and his free gift with the undeserved kindness by the one man Jesus Christ abounded much more to many. So, then, as through one trespass the result to men of all sorts was condemnation, likewise also through one act of justification the result to men of all sorts is a declaring of them righteous for life."—Romans 5:15, 18.

[9] Thus, there is a perfect balancing of these vital matters. The one committing the "one trespass" was the first man on earth, Adam. The "one act of justification" was performed by the only other perfect man, Jesus. This allowed for him to become the "Eternal Father" of the descendants of the trespassing Adam. In this way he becomes a second Adam toward the human family. The sacrifice of his perfect human life and the presenting of that human life-right to the Great Judge in

---

8. Why was Jesus enabled to take action to become the "Eternal Father" to mankind, and how was this confirmed by the apostle Paul?

9. How did Jesus become a second Adam to mankind, but from what realm does he act as mankind's Father?

Christ, in kingly power, becomes the "Eternal Father" to all those whom he adopts

heaven make it impossible for him to serve here on earth as an eternal father of mankind. When he was resurrected from the dead, he was returned to the spirit realm and was exalted to his Resurrector's right hand. Thus it is stated: "It is even so written: 'The first man Adam became a living soul.' The last Adam became a life-giving spirit." (1 Corinthians 15:45) Mankind's new, adoptive Father will give it the best start in life possible.

The First Human Creatures to Be Fathered

10 The "Eternal Father," Jesus Christ the King, will demonstrate who are the first ones to be fathered by him. How? By preserving through "the great tribulation" the dedicated lives of millions now living. They are the "great crowd" of "other sheep."—Revelation 7:9, 14.

---

10. Who are the first human creatures to be fathered by this adoptive Father?

[11] Unparalleled is the earthly opportunity that is set before the "great crowd" after "the great tribulation." Described as part of "the sign" of this "conclusion of the system of things," the figurative goats of Jesus' parable will be cut off from life on this earth, which will mean everlasting destruction for them. But not so the "great crowd" of sheeplike ones who lovingly and loyally did good to the remnant of Christ's spiritual "brothers" yet on earth. (Matthew 25:31-46) The

11. What earthly opportunity lies before the sheeplike survivors of "the great tribulation"?

preservation of such "sheep" clear to the other side of "the great tribulation" and into the Millennial Reign of the foretold "Prince of Peace" will make it possible for these survivors to enter into the blessings of the Kingdom realm. They will be the earthly subjects of the "Prince of Peace."

[12] At that time the words that Jesus spoke before he raised Lazarus from the dead will be fulfilled toward those who enter the Kingdom's earthly realm. He said: "I am the resurrection and the life. He that exercises faith in me, even though he dies, will come to life; and everyone that is living and exercises faith in me will never die at all." (John 11:25, 26) For their obedience to him, they will attain to perfect human life in the King's earthly realm. Even the sympathetic evildoer who died alongside Jesus at Calvary will be favored with the opportunity of entering the Paradise. (Luke 23:43) Jesus will live up to all that his name "Eternal Father" implies.

The Happy Prospect for the Dead

[13] Jesus, the most outstanding descendant of Abraham, said that this forefather, his son Isaac, and his grandson Jacob would be seen in the earthly realm of God's Kingdom. (Matthew 22: 31, 32) This would be made possible by the resurrection. As Jesus said, all the human dead in the

---

12. What words of Jesus about the resurrection indicate that endless life is set before those who enter the Kingdom's earthly realm?

13. The resurrection of the human dead will make it possible for what noted persons of ancient times to be seen in the earthly realm of the Kingdom?

memorial tombs will hear the voice of the Son of God and come forth. Their future thereafter will depend upon the course of action that they take. —John 5:28, 29; Revelation 20:12-15.

[14] Tremendous preparations will have to be made for the ones of mankind who will be brought up from the grave to life on earth under the Kingdom of the "Eternal Father." These preparations will first be undertaken by the survivors of "the war of the great day of God the Almighty" at Armageddon. (Revelation 16:14, 16) How many in number the "great crowd" of the "other sheep" of the "Prince of Peace" will have become by that time we do not now know, but there will be enough for the task.

[15] Psalm 45 is addressed to this "Prince of Peace" as King, and since he is to be to mankind the "Eternal Father," this psalm says to him: "In place of your forefathers there will come to be your sons, whom you will appoint as princes in all the earth." (Psalm 45:16) But even before the resurrection of those faithful "forefathers," male members of the "great crowd" of Armageddon survivors will have been appointed to such princely office. Thousands of these prospective survivors of Armageddon are already serving as elders in the more than 49,000 congregations of Jehovah's Witnesses, superintending the spiritual interests of their respective congregations.

---

14. What will have to be done in advance in behalf of those in line for the earthly resurrection, and who will be the ones to share first in these preparations?
15. Many will serve in what special capacity under the adoptive Father of mankind?

[16] Under princely supervision, the Armageddon survivors will serve with zealous cooperation. Just what instructions the "princes in all the earth" will receive from the heavenly "Prince of Peace" remains to be seen, furnishing a thrilling experience for all their fellow survivors of Armageddon. Think of all the garments that will have to be prepared to clothe the returning dead in suitable attire! Think of all the food supplies that will have to be provided or laid up in store! Places of shelter will also need to be made ready. What an exciting time that will be for all those engaged in this preparatory work! Who will come back first? Will they come back in the reverse order from that in which they went down into the memorial tombs? Will the martyr Abel and Enoch, who was taken away by God, as well as Noah, Abraham, Isaac, Jacob, and all the faithful prophets, be specially rewarded by being resurrected first?

[17] The "Prince of Peace" knows and will determine this. And he will be fully competent for his responsibilities as the new Father of redeemed mankind. Another of his foretold titles was "Mighty God." That signifies that he is to be a mighty, powerful One. The demonstration of his godship will be mighty in that he will resurrect all the ransomed dead, remembering their individual names and their personalities. (John 5:28, 29; Acts 10:42) He is perfectly able to undo all the

---

16. (a) Under princely supervision, the Armageddon survivors will serve in what activity? (b) What questions arise as to the order in which the dead will return?
17. Who will determine the order in which the dead will return to life on earth, and what title foretold concerning him indicates his ability to handle his responsibilities?

damage that Satan the Devil has done during the past 6,000 years of human existence.

18 The first Adam bequeathed a condemnation to death to all his offspring. Did Adam become the forefather of the man Jesus Christ? No, Jesus did not have a human father but was born from a virgin made pregnant with his life-force that God transferred from the spirit realm. So the sinner Adam did not become a forefather of that earthly Son of God. The second Adam, however, has become a life-giving spirit. In this capacity he can fulfill Isaiah's prophecy and become the "Eternal Father" to the first Adam's offspring, whom he repurchases and adopts for the purpose of bestowing perfect human life on a paradise earth.

19 In such a way the heavenly Father of Jesus Christ will become the heavenly Grandfather of the restored human family. For this reason the human family will enter into a new relationship with the Creator of heaven and earth. Never was there the least possibility that Jehovah would fail in his original purpose. Thus Jehovah will have foiled the vicious, ungodly scheme of Satan the Devil. All the repurchased human family will be brought to the knowledge of this fact. What a wonderful day it will be when Jesus Christ takes over the fatherhood of the human family in order to rear mankind in Paradise restored to earth!

---

18. (a) How was the need for Adam to become the forefather of Jesus Christ obviated? (b) How was Jesus enabled to become a second father to Adam's offspring?
19. Into what new relationship toward the human race will Jehovah God come, and what scheme of Satan the Devil will he thus foil?

Chapter 21

The Garden of Eden Restored—Earth Wide

THE GARDEN of Eden was "a paradise of pleasure," and in that sense it will be restored. (Genesis 2:8, *Douay Version*) The original Paradise covered a limited area of the globe. But Jehovah purposed that its borders were to be extended outward, all around, by the growing human family until Paradise enveloped the entire earth and enrobed it with exquisite natural beauty. (Genesis 1:26-28; 2:8, 9, 15) Jesus' words to the sympathetic evildoer who died alongside him at Calvary assured the man that he would be resurrected when the restoration of Paradise is well along, and he will then notice the delightful change in the earthly scene. (Luke 23:43) What will the restored global Paradise be like? How will it be different from the original garden of Eden?

2 In the entrancing prophecies of glorious things that are just ahead, we do see something missing from the restored, earth-wide Paradise. What is that? It is "the tree of the knowledge of

1. (a) In what sense will the garden of Eden be restored, and why will it not cover only a limited area of the globe? (b) What do Jesus' words to the evildoer indicate?
2. (a) What was in the original garden of Eden that will be missing from the earth-wide Paradise? (b) Why is it reasonable that God will not test mankind's obedience by means of a single tree?

good and bad" that was "in the middle of the garden." (Genesis 2:17; 3:3) This was evidently a single tree. Would it be reasonable to think that in the middle of the restored, earth-wide garden of Eden there should be such a single tree upon which there would be a divine prohibition? No. It would require a tremendous amount of traveling for people in the far corners of the earth to go to the location of such a tree in the Middle East so as possibly to eat fruit from it in disobedience to the Most High God.

[3] Moreover, there will not be at such a location a "talking" serpent to invite those who approach the tree to partake of its attractive-looking fruit out of sheer spite for God's orders. And there will not be any invisible wicked spirit to manipulate a serpent and make it appear to talk and to invite the beholder to rebel against God by adopting a course of disobedience to the Creator, with fatal consequences.

[4] No, the invisible spirit creature that was behind the "talking" serpent back there in the garden of Eden will not be on hand during the Millennial Reign of the "Prince of Peace," Christ Jesus. That wicked one, Satan the Devil, will be put under complete restraint after Armageddon. Revelation 20:2, 3 tells us that the "Prince of Peace" will seize "the original serpent, who is the Devil and Satan," and bind him and hurl him into the abyss for a thousand years.

---

3. What else will be missing from the restored Paradise?
4. Why will Satan the Devil not be on hand during the Thousand Year Reign of the "Prince of Peace"?

True Peace and Security in the Restored Paradise

5 What peace and security will follow! Gone will be Satan's influence and domination over mankind as "the ruler of the world"! (John 14:30) With Satan's hordes of demons also abyssed, the earth will at last be free of all kinds of spiritism,

---

5. In the restored Paradise, why will true peace and security prevail earth wide?

A literal paradise will beautify all of God's "footstool," the earth

occultism, and black magic—yes, every form of demonism, which Jehovah detests.—Deuteronomy 18:10-12.

[6] The animal creation will not do injury or be any threat to the dwellers in the restored Para-

---

6, 7. (a) Why will the animal creation not be any threat to humans? (b) What prophecy in this regard will have a literal fulfillment?

dise. God will return to the lower creatures any lost measure of fear of humans. Thus we can look for the charming description of animal life that is set out in Isaiah 11:6-9 to have a literal fulfillment during the Millennial Reign of the "Prince of Peace":

7 "The wolf will actually reside for a while with the male lamb, and with the kid the leopard itself will lie down, and the calf and the maned young lion and the well-fed animal all together; and a mere little boy will be leader over them. And the cow and the bear themselves will feed; together their young ones will lie down. And even the lion will eat straw just like the bull. And the sucking child will certainly play upon the hole of the cobra; and upon the light aperture of a poisonous snake will a weaned child actually put his own hand. They will not do any harm or cause any ruin in all my holy mountain; because the earth will certainly be filled with the knowledge of Jehovah as the waters are covering the very sea."

8 It would be inconsistent for God to inspire such a prophecy to have only a spiritual meaning and not to reflect such things in actual earthly life. Similarly, Isaiah 65:25 tells us: "The wolf and the lamb themselves will feed as one, and the lion will eat straw just like the bull; and as for the serpent, his food will be dust." Does this signify the annihilation of the serpent family out of the global garden of Eden? No, the prophetic statement that the serpent's food "will be dust" means

---

8. What is meant by the prophetic statement that the serpent's food "will be dust"?

that members of the reptile family will never again be a menace to the life and good health of human creatures. They will have to recognize that humankind is their master who has dominion over everything that moves upon the earth, just as was the case of Adam in the garden of Eden when he named all the animals without fear. —Genesis 2:19, 20; Hosea 2:18.

[9] The beauty and abundance of that earth-wide garden of Eden is beyond our imagination. But the Bible does give us a prophetic description of it in the 65th psalm, addressed to God. In part, this psalm says: "You have turned your attention to the earth, that you may give it abundance; you enrich it very much. The stream from God is full of water. You prepare their grain, for that is the way you prepare the earth." No droughts then but, rather, "copious showers"! (Psalm 65:1, 9-13) There will be an abundance of food for all earth's inhabitants.

[10] This abundance is also foretold at Isaiah 25:6: "Jehovah of armies will certainly make for all the peoples, in this mountain, a banquet of well-oiled dishes, a banquet of wine kept on the dregs." The inhabitants of the restored Paradise will eat well-oiled dishes that sustain the heart and make the face shine. They will drink wine, well aged on the dregs and filtered, making their hearts glad. (Psalm 104:14, 15) No food shortages under the Millennial Reign of the "Prince of Peace"! Instead, there will be "an overflow."—Psalm 72:16.

9, 10. What do Psalm 65 and Isaiah 25:6 foretell about the earth under the reign of the "Prince of Peace"?

Changes in Language and in Weather

11 Will the earth-wide Paradise suffer from the confusion of having many languages? No, because the "Prince of Peace" is also referred to as the "Mighty God." (Isaiah 9:6) Thus he is able to reverse the confusion of language that began at the Tower of Babel. (Genesis 11:6-9) What will become the common language of all the earthly children of the "Eternal Father"? Will it be the original language of the first Adam, the language with which Jehovah endowed him? Likely. In any event, all language barriers will be wiped out. You will be able to travel anywhere and communicate with people. You will be able to understand them, and they will be able to understand you. There will be one language for all mankind, and it would be appropriate for the entire Bible to be available in that language. (Compare Zephaniah 3:9.) In that language all the earth will be filled with the knowledge of Jehovah "as the waters are covering the very sea."—Isaiah 11:9.

12 Fulfilled then will be the words of Zechariah 14:9: "In that day Jehovah will prove to be one, and his name one." Jehovah alone will be worshiped as the one true God. In "that day" of Jehovah's Kingdom by the "Prince of Peace," God will reveal the exact pronunciation of his name. Then there will be just one pronunciation of that holy name by everybody on earth. His name will be one.

---

11. What change in language will take place, and how will this affect mankind?
12. How will Zechariah 14:9 experience a fulfillment?

[13] What weather and environmental changes there will be are also a matter of keen interest to those looking forward to the global Paradise of the "Prince of Peace." One thing is certain: The whole earth will be made an exquisite place in which to live. Never will that Paradise be disturbed by destructive storms, tornadoes, tidal waves, hurricanes, or typhoons. Wind, waves, and weather will all obey the "Prince of Peace." (Mark 4:37-41) The global garden of Eden will have complete weather control. All the earth will be beautified into a paradise of pleasure, where it will be the happy privilege of all mankind to dwell securely to time without end.

[14] No reason for any tears of sorrow then! Jehovah's prophetic Word assures us: "The tent of God is with mankind, and he will reside with them, and they will be his peoples. And God himself will be with them. And he will wipe out every tear from their eyes, and death will be no more, neither will mourning nor outcry nor pain be anymore."—Revelation 21:3, 4.

[15] The heavens are God's throne, and the earth is his footstool. (Isaiah 66:1) So God cannot dwell on the earth in a literal sense. But he will tent with mankind. During the Thousand Year Reign, Jehovah will tent among mankind representatively by his glorified Son, Jesus Christ. How apt it is that Jehovah's presence will be represented by his

---

13. Why will weather, wind, and waves pose no threat to earth's inhabitants?

14, 15. (a) What promise recorded at Revelation 21:3, 4 will be fulfilled? (b) How will God tent among mankind? (c) What kind of tears will be wiped out forever?

"Prince of Peace"! This brings to mind the words of Isaiah 7:14 about the name applied to the Messiah—Immanuel. That name means "With Us Is God." (Matthew 1:23) How thrilling that, by means of his dearest Son, God will "reside" with mankind! Then tears of joy will likely come into our eyes as we see the marvelous miracles performed by this "Mighty God," especially when dead loved ones are brought back to life in the resurrection to Paradise conditions. (Acts 24:15) Such miracles will be marvelous evidence that God is with mankind and that he is wiping out all the sorrowful tears from our eyes forever.

A Beauty Spot in the Boundless Universe

16 The first Adam was told how to start off the project of extending Paradise from right there in the garden of Eden. The accomplishment of that original purpose to extend it earth wide will be realized. But will the resurrection of the dead have to wait until the Paradise extends all around the globe? No. For example, those who come back in an early resurrection will be resurrected into the portions of the earth where the Armageddon survivors are and have converted such areas into a paradise. As the resurrection of mankind in general progresses, these Paradise areas will expand until they join to form the earth-wide Paradise.

17 The Paradise to come will surpass all the lovely parks or gardens today. Radiantly, the entire

16. Does the resurrection of the dead have to wait till Paradise is extended to cover the globe? Explain.
17. What description is given of the global Paradise?

earth will bloom as a peaceful paradise, one that delights not only the eye of men but even the eye of the Creator. It will be a global garden of Eden adorned with vegetation and trees—good to look at and producing food for sustaining creature life in perfection. The earth will forever remain a beauty spot in all of Jehovah's boundless universe. And all unified mankind will have the everlasting obligation and privilege to keep the earth such a beauty spot.

[18] All members of this godly human family will dwell together peaceably as brothers and sisters in all purity, for they will actually be children of the "Eternal Father," the "Prince of Peace." So there will be no arrogant dominating on the part of men over women, their sisters. But the perfected women will be what Jehovah God purposes, even as he purposed Eve to be "a helper for" her perfect husband, Adam.—Genesis 2:18; see also 1 Peter 3:7.

[19] The sight that the paradisaic earth filled with perfect men and women will then present to those in the invisible heavens will be far grander and lovelier than the appearance of the earth when first created, at which time "the morning stars joyfully cried out together, and all the sons of God began shouting in applause." (Job 38:7) Then the Most High God, Jehovah, will have been fully vindicated as the One whose glorious purpose can never be defeated. All praise to him!

---

18. How do we know that all, men and women, will dwell together peaceably as brothers and sisters?

19. The Paradise earth will present what sight to those who dwell in the invisible heavens?

Chapter 22

The God of the "Prince of Peace" Becomes "All Things to Everyone"

SHORTLY after his resurrection, the "Prince of Peace" said to one of his disciples: "I am ascending to my Father and your Father and to my God and your God." (John 20:17) With those words he acknowledged that his heavenly Father was also his God, the One alone whom he worshiped. In such worship he set an example for all other creatures throughout heaven and earth.

2 What a grand example the "Prince of Peace" will become to all perfected humankind when he loyally submits himself in a special way to the One who is the ideal Sovereign of all the universe! This will be matchlessly revealed at the close of his Thousand Year Reign over mankind, when he will have restored peace, security, and harmony to all the earth. In an unerring prophecy, we are assured of this:

3 "Next, the end, when he hands over the kingdom to his God and Father, when he has brought to nothing all government and all authority and

---

1. In what does Jesus Christ set an example for all other creatures in heaven and on earth?

2, 3. (a) How does 1 Corinthians 15:24-26, 28 describe Jesus' special act of subjection to his Father? (b) What will be the grand result?

power. For he must rule as king until God has put all enemies under his feet. As the last enemy, death is to be brought to nothing. But when all things will have been subjected to him, then the Son himself will also subject himself to the One who subjected all things to him, that God may be all things to everyone." (1 Corinthians 15: 24-26, 28) Or as *The Amplified Bible* renders the latter part of verse 28: "So that God may be all in all—that is, be everything to everyone, supreme, the indwelling and controlling factor of life."

4 When the "Prince of Peace" hands over the Kingdom to his God at the end of the Thousand Year Reign, earth's inhabitants will be made aware of this act of their adoptive Father. With him as their Royal Example, they will likewise subject themselves in a new aspect to the Most High God. Now for the first time they will render loving submission directly to Jehovah, yes, worship, in all sincerity and truth, no longer requiring the priestly services of Jesus, not even when praying.

5 In this manner the Most High God again becomes King of all the universe with no royal representative for him either in heaven or on earth. It follows that the 144,000 associate kings whom Jesus Christ has redeemed from the earth will also bend the knee before the supreme Royal Ruler and will in this added sense acknowledge him to be the Universal Sovereign.

---

4. (a) How will earth's inhabitants respond to the example of their adoptive Father? (b) What new aspect of submission will then exist?
5. What will be the attitude of the 144,000 associate kings of Jesus Christ?

Final Test Upon All Mankind

6 Recognizing Jehovah as the Supreme Judge, Jesus Christ desires that the all-necessary divine approval be expressed upon the work that Jesus has accomplished during his Millennial Rule. During that rule, those humans who refused to conform to the requirements of righteousness and who showed disobedience to the King will have been destroyed. Thus, those whom Jesus Christ turns over to Jehovah God, the final Judge, will be those obedient ones who have attained to human perfection.

7 At that point it is time for the enduring nature of human devotion with regard to the Universal Sovereign, Jehovah God, to be put to the test. As in the case of Job, the question is: Do they love and worship God only for all the good things that he has done for them, or do they love him because of what he is in his very own self—the Rightful Sovereign of the universe? (Job 1:8-11) But how will perfected mankind be put to a test of heart allegiance? The Bible answers: Satan the Devil and his demons will be loosed "for a little while" from the abyss in which they have been confined for a thousand years. (Revelation 20:3) By permitting the Devil to put restored mankind to the test, members of perfected mankind can be proved as to

---

6. (a) What will happen to disobedient humans during Jesus' Millennial Rule? (b) What will be the state of those whom Jesus turns over to his heavenly Father?
7. (a) What will be put to a searching test after Jesus hands back the Kingdom? (b) How will perfected mankind be put to that test?

their individual integrity to God in a perfect sense. —Compare Job 1:12.

[8] Seven thousand years previously, Satan the Devil was able to induce the perfect Adam and Eve to sin by taking a self-seeking course of action. What methods of temptation Jehovah will permit Satan and the demons to employ after their release from the abyss the Scriptures do not say. But no doubt there will be an appeal to selfishness and to a desire for independence from God. Still a rebel himself against Jehovah's sovereignty, the Devil will be intent on making rebels of mankind too. Exactly to what degree these released demonic forces will be successful is also not stated, but there will be enough human rebels to make an impression as of a large crowd. Sin on the part of any human creature, now perfected, will then be intelligently undertaken and, therefore, be deliberate, willful. It will signify departure from the worship of the only true and living God and a taking of the side of Satan the Devil. (Revelation 20:7, 8) Thus, in the case of these rebellious ones, Jehovah does not become "all things to everyone."

[9] The loyal ones, however, refuse to give in to the arguments and pressures of the misled, nationalistic ones. Unhesitatingly, the loyal ones choose to let Jehovah be "all things to everyone" in their own

---

8. (a) Upon being released from the abyss, what will Satan and his demons endeavor to do? (b) Those who allow themselves to be misled by the Devil and his demons will be taking what course of action?

9. (a) What will happen to those who do not keep integrity to Jehovah God? (b) How will the invisible realm be rid of all rebels? (c) What grand condition will then prevail throughout heaven and earth?

case. For justice itself, Jehovah's sovereignty must be strictly enforced. Consequently, all the satanically influenced rebels on earth will be wiped out of existence forever. Good riddance to them! The invisible realm of creation must also be rid of all rebels. So, to bring the universal purification to completion, Satan the Devil and all his demon hordes will be annihilated, blotted out of existence. Thus the heavens and the earth will be cleansed of every taint of sin. (Revelation 20:9, 10) Jehovah's holiness will prevail everywhere. (Compare Zechariah 14:20.) The sacred name of the Most High Deity will be sanctified in heaven and on earth. All who live in heaven and on earth will joyfully do his supreme will.

[10] To all eternity our earth will bear a distinction that no other planet throughout endless space will enjoy, though the earth may not be the only planet that will ever be inhabited. Uniquely, it will be where Jehovah has indisputably vindicated his universal sovereignty, establishing an eternal and universal legal precedent. It will be the only planet on which Jehovah of armies will have fought "the war of the great day of God the Almighty." It will be the only planet to which God sent his dearest Son to become a man and die in order to recover the planet's inhabitants from sin and death. It will be the only planet from which Jehovah will have taken 144,000 of its inhabitants to be "heirs indeed of God, but joint heirs with Christ."—Romans 8:17.

---

10. In what ways will the earth for all eternity bear a distinction that no other planet will enjoy?

Seraphs, Cherubs, Angels

[11] God, the glorious Source of all creation, celestial and terrestrial, will become "all things" not only to the 144,000 heirs with Christ but also to others in the heavenly realm. In chapter 6 of the book of Isaiah, we are given a glimpse into the heavenly courts. There we read: "I, however, got to see Jehovah, sitting on a throne lofty and lifted up, and his skirts were filling the temple. Seraphs were standing above him. Each one had six wings. With two he kept his face covered, and with two he kept his feet covered, and with two he would fly about. And this one called to that one and said: 'Holy, holy, holy is Jehovah of armies. The fullness of all the earth is his glory.'"—Isaiah 6:1-3.

[12] How highly favored Isaiah was to see the holiest One in all the universe seated upon his celestial throne attended by glorious seraphs! What an awesome vision that was, revealing the highly favored position that those seraphs occupied, for he is the All Holy One whose sacredness they acclaimed as they testified to his holiness by emphasizing it in a threefold way! The seraphs are interested in helping Jehovah's worshipers to be holy as God is holy.—Isaiah 6:5-7.

[13] Just as there is a variety of creature life down here on earth, bespeaking the power of Jehovah God, so there are also creatures of another kind in

---

11, 12. (a) What kind of spirit creatures did Isaiah see in a vision? (b) What interest do these have in us humans?

13. (a) What other kind of spirit creatures does the Bible reveal to us? (b) How is Jehovah described in relation to them?

the spirit realm. The Bible discloses that these are the glorious cherubs, who must be very speedy in flight. (Psalm 18:10; compare Hebrews 9:4, 5.) Genesis 3:24 shows that after Adam and Eve had sinned against the holy God of heaven by partaking of the forbidden fruit, the Creator posted to the east of the way back into the Paradise of pleasure the cherubs along with "the flaming blade of a sword that was turning itself continually." Jehovah is spoken of as "sitting upon the cherubs." (Psalm 99:1; Isaiah 37:16) Thus he is shown to throne above the cherubs.

[14] Not to be overlooked among the multitude of spirit creatures are the angels. There are many millions of them. (Daniel 7:9, 10) Among them are the angels assigned to minister to Jehovah's worshipers on earth. Jesus warned that no one should stumble any of Jehovah's worshipers for the reason that "their angels in heaven always behold the face of my Father who is in heaven." (Matthew 18:10; Hebrews 1:14) At the end of Jesus' 40 days of fasting in the wilderness and after his victoriously resisting the three crucial temptations presented by the Devil, what a privilege it was for the angels to minister to the physical needs of the lean, hungry Jesus!—Matthew 4:11.

[15] Up in the heavenly realm, the glorious spir-

14. (a) What other kind of spirit creatures are not to be overlooked? (b) How numerous are they?
15, 16. (a) Describe the familylike unity that will exist in heaven and on earth. (b) What reward from Jehovah will be given to those perfected humans who pass the test successfully? (c) How will Jehovah look upon the attainment of his original purpose?

it inhabitants will be brothers to one another, whereas down here on the earth the perfected human family will be made brothers and sisters to one another. They will be in the image and likeness of God to the grand extent that Adam and Eve, fresh from the creative hands of Jehovah God, were in the 'image and likeness' of their Creator. (Genesis 1:26, 27) After passing the final test, the perfected humans will be granted the right to live forever and will lovingly be adopted as "the children of God," rejoicing in glorious freedom, and become part of Jehovah's united family in heaven and on earth.—Romans 8:21.

[16] With what pleasure and exultation of his entire being Jehovah God will look upon the attainment of his original purpose—the matchless feat of having all things according to his primordial determination—all creatures in an unbreakable loving unity with him!

[17] In the light of all of this, who will be able to refrain from blessing this wonderful divine Purposer? Not improperly lifting up his words of address to superhuman creatures, the psalmist says: "Bless Jehovah, O you angels of his, mighty in power, carrying out his word, by listening to the voice of his word. Bless Jehovah, all you armies of his, you ministers of his, doing his will."—Psalm 103:20, 21.

[18] The elated, inspired psalmist concludes the book of Psalms with these words of exhortation:

---

17. In view of all of this, who will be able to refrain from doing what, in harmony with the words of the psalmist?
18. How does the psalmist conclude the book of Psalms?

“Praise Jah, you people! Praise God in his holy place. Praise him in the expanse of his strength. Praise him for his works of mightiness. Praise him according to the abundance of his greatness. Praise him with the blowing of the horn. Praise him with the stringed instrument and the harp. Praise him with the tambourine and the circle dance. Praise him with strings and the pipe. Praise him with the cymbals of melodious sound. Praise him with the clashing cymbals. Every breathing thing—let it praise Jah. Praise Jah, you people!”
—Psalm 150:1-6.

The entire universe will be united in peaceful worship of the Universal Sovereign

[19] The entire universe will be united at last in a perfect bond that will hold for eternity, the bond of the one worship of the heavenly Father because his children love and adore him above all. Yes, then it will be that all intelligent creatures will say, in effect, as the seraphs said: "Holy, holy, holy is Jehovah of armies. The fullness of all the earth is his glory." Then, indeed, the God of the "Prince of Peace" will have become "all things to everyone" —forever and ever.

19. (a) In what bond will the universe then be united? (b) What will all intelligent creatures, in effect, say?

CHIEF OFFICE AND OFFICIAL ADDRESS OF
Watch Tower Bible and Tract Society of Pennsylvania
Watchtower Bible and Tract Society of New York, Inc.
International Bible Students Association
25 Columbia Heights, Brooklyn, New York 11201, U.S.A.

ADDRESSES OF BRANCH OFFICES:

ALASKA 99507: 2552 East 48th Ave., Anchorage. **ARGENTINA:** Caldas 1551, 1427 Buenos Aires. **AUSTRALIA:** Box 280, Ingleburn, N.S.W. 2565; Zouch Road, Denham Court, N.S.W. 2565. **AUSTRIA:** Gallgasse 44, A-1130 Vienna. **BAHAMAS:** Box N-1247, Nassau, N.P. **BARBADOS:** Fontabelle Rd., Bridgetown. **BELGIUM:** rue d'Argile 60, B-1950 Kraainem. **BELIZE:** Box 257, Belize City. **BOLIVIA:** Casilla No. 1440, La Paz. **BRAZIL:** Rodovia SP-141, Km 43, 18280 Cesario Lange, SP; Caixa Postal 92, 18270 Tatuí, SP. **BURMA:** P.O. Box 62, Rangoon. **CANADA L7G 4Y4:** Box 4100, Halton Hills (Georgetown), Ontario. **CHILE:** Av. Concha y Toro 3456, Puente Alto; Casilla 267, Puente Alto. **COLOMBIA:** Apartado Aereo 85058, Bogotá 8, D.E. **COSTA RICA:** Apartado 10043, San José. **CYPRUS:** P. O. Box 4091, Limassol. **DENMARK:** P.B. 340; Stenhusvej 28, DK-4300 Holbæk. **DOMINICAN REPUBLIC:** Avenida Francia 33 (Apartado 1742), Santo Domingo. **ECUADOR:** Casilla 4512, Guayaquil. **EL SALVADOR:** Apartado 401, San Salvador. **ENGLAND NW7 1RN:** The Ridgeway, London. **FIJI:** Box 23, Suva. **FINLAND:** Postbox 68, SF-01301 Vantaa 30. **FRANCE:** 81 rue du Point-du-Jour, F-92100 Boulogne-Billancourt. **GERMANY, FEDERAL REPUBLIC OF:** Postfach 20, D-6251 Selters/Taunus 1. **GHANA:** Box 760, Accra. **GREECE:** 77 Leoforos Kifisias, GR-151 24 Marousi. **GUADELOUPE:** B.P. 239, 97156 Pointe-à-Pitre Cedex. **GUAM 96913:** 143 Jehovah St., Barrigada. **GUATEMALA:** 11 Avenida 5-67, Guatemala 1. **GUYANA:** 50 Brickdam, Georgetown 16. **HAITI:** Post Box 185, Port-au-Prince. **HAWAII 96814:** 1228 Pensacola St., Honolulu. **HONDURAS:** Apartado 147, Tegucigalpa. **HONG KONG:** 4 Kent Road, Kowloon Tong. **ICELAND:** P. O. Box 8496, IS-128 Reykjavík. **INDIA:** Post Bag 10, Lonavla, Pune Dis., Mah. 410 401. **IRELAND:** 29A Jamestown Road, Finglas, Dublin 11. **ISRAEL:** P. O. Box 961, 61-009 Tel Aviv. **ITALY:** Via della Bufalotta 1281, I-00138 Rome RM. **IVORY COAST:** 06 B.P. 393, Abidjan 06. **JAMAICA:** Box 180, Kingston 10. **JAPAN:** 1271 Nakashinden, Ebina City, Kanagawa Pref., 243-04. **KENYA:** Box 47788, Nairobi. **KOREA, REPUBLIC OF:** Box 33 Pyungtaek P. O., Kyunggido, 180. **LEEWARD ISLANDS:** Box 119, St. Johns, Antigua. **LIBERIA:** P.O. Box 171, Monrovia. **LUXEMBOURG:** 15, rue de l'Egalite, L-1456 Luxembourg, G D. **MALAYSIA:** 28 Jalan Kampar, Off Jalan Landasan, 41300 Klang, Sel. **MARTINIQUE:** Cours Campeche, Morne Tartenson, 97200 Fort de France. **MAURITIUS:** 22 Dr. Roux St., Rose Hill. **MEXICO:** Apartado Postal 42-048, 06470 México, D.F. **NETHERLANDS:** Noordbargerstraat 77, 7812 AA Emmen. **NETHERLANDS ANTILLES:** Oosterbeekstraat 11, Willemstad, Curaçao. **NEW CALEDONIA:** B.P. 787, Nouméa. **NEW ZEALAND:** P.O. Box 142; 198 Mahia Rd., Manurewa. **NIGERIA:** P.O. Box 194, Yaba, Lagos State. **NORWAY:** Gaupeveien 24, N-1914 Ytre Enebakk. **PAKISTAN:** 197-A Ahmad Block, New Garden Town, Lahore 16. **PANAMA:** Apartado 1835, Panama 9A. **PAPUA NEW GUINEA:** Box 113, Port Moresby. **PERU:** Av. El Cortijo 329, Monterrico Chico, Lima 33; Casilla 5178, Miraflores, Lima 18. **PHILIPPINES, REPUBLIC OF:** P.O. Box 2044, Manila 2800; 186 Roosevelt Ave., San Francisco del Monte, Quezon City 3010. **PORTUGAL:** Av. D. Nuno Álvares Pereira, 11, P-2765 Estoril. **PUERTO RICO 00927:** Calle Onix 23, Urb. Bucaré, Río Piedras. **SENEGAL:** B.P. 3107, Dakar. **SIERRA LEONE:** P. O. Box 136, Freetown. **SOLOMON ISLANDS:** P.O. Box 166, Honiara. **SOUTH AFRICA:** Private Bag 2, Elandsfontein, 1406. **SPAIN:** Apartado postal 132, Torrejón de Ardoz (Madrid). **SRI LANKA, REP. OF:** 62 Layard's Road, Colombo 5. **SURINAME:** Wicherstraat 8-10; Box 49, Paramaribo. **SWEDEN:** Box 5, S-732 00 Arboga. **SWITZERLAND:** Ulmenweg 45; P.O. Box 225, CH-3602 Thun. **TAHITI:** B.P. 518, Papeete. **TAIWAN:** 109 Yun Ho Street, Taipei 10613. **THAILAND:** 69/1 Soi 2, Sukhumwit Rd., Bangkok 10 110. **TRINIDAD:** Lower Rapsey Street & Laxmi Lane, Curepe. **UNITED STATES OF AMERICA:** 25 Columbia Heights, Brooklyn, N.Y. 11201. **URUGUAY:** Francisco Bauzá 3372, Montevideo. **VENEZUELA:** Apartado 116, La Victoria, Edo. Aragua 2121A. **WESTERN SAMOA:** P. O. Box 673, Apia. **ZAIRE, REP. OF:** B.P. 634, Limete, Kinshasa. **ZAMBIA, REP. OF:** Box 21598, Kitwe. **ZIMBABWE:** 35 Fife Avenue, Harare.